Tomorrow Brings

This is a work of nonfiction. The names and certain identifying characteristics of many individuals described in this book have been changed.

Tomorrow Brings / Frank G.

ISBN 978-0-6151-6010-8

For Thomas, Crystal, Adam, Jadon, and Joey –

You give me reason to live. I love you all.

FG, 2007

Dear Mr. V,

We accept the fact that we had to sacrifice a whole Saturday in detention for whatever it was we did wrong. But we think you're crazy to make an essay telling you who we think we are. You see us as you want to see us... In the simplest terms, in the most convenient definitions.

But what we found out is that each one of us is a brain...

...and an athlete...

...and a basket case...

-- a princess...

-- and a criminal...

Does that answer your question?

Sincerely yours,

T.B.C.

It starts again with that feeling deep in my stomach. It's usually the feeling that something is about to go horribly wrong. Then again, it could be something wonderful. That's a symptom of a greater problem -- that my brain can't tell the difference. I spend more time anticipating bad things than good. I feel like I've slowly trapped myself by not realizing what was happening. I made a long chain of decisions that caused things to get worse and worse -- each time thinking I was doing something to improve the situation, of course. So, where did it all start? To what point can I trace this all back? To answer that, one needs more info.

Not being able to read body language or pick up on signals is not something you can be aware of from within. Think about it for a second. If you're unable to comprehend the things people are saying via non-verbal methods, how much communication would you miss out on? It's frustration supreme from this end! If I had a nickel for every time I heard, "Could you stop mumbling? I can't understand you!" I'd be as rich as that cliche is old. Seriously, I'm NOT mumbling. That's just as loud as I get. Spend a lifetime worrying what people will say if they hear your voice - that you'll screw up and say something stupid - that you'll say something the wrong way and people will make fun of you. Top that off with a constant concern about your looks, weight, height, grooming, and whatever else concerns people about their appearance and you begin to scratch the surface of what it's been like in my head for 30 years.

Did it start that day in 7th grade, when the two stuck up girls were picking on the new fat kid in class?

Alone in yet another new school, 2000 miles away from home? Playing with his hair, whispering and blowing in his ear? I can tell you the bitter end of that screwed up conversation verbatim, 20 years later:

"Heyyy...have you got a girlfriend yet?"

"No...and I don't WANT one, either! Leave me alone!"

Smooth, eh? Now, I will always maintain the two of them were screwing with me, as that was what they did. There's always one voice that asks "What if they were serious and you blew it right there?" I was young - I skipped a grade so I started middle school at 11 and quite honestly didn't care about girls yet. Dragons, superheroes, books – those were still my interests at that point. We had just moved for the second time in a year, across the country from everything I knew and most everyone I loved. I was truly all alone in that world. I had no peers to relate to. An outburst like that *in front of everyone* had inadvertently set the tone for the remainder of my school years.

The voices were already there, of course. I didn't know they were unique or special though. I always assumed EVERYONE heard that stuff. Let's get this straight right now: I don't HEAR them out loud. I don't SEE things, or imagine things that aren't there.

I have no "imaginary friends" (or enemies.) There are *no multiple personalities* involved (that's an entirely different problem from which I thankfully don't suffer.) *That* stuff is media driven misconception at it's finest -- made up by Hollywood to more easily explain a non-visual concept.

No, what I have are *several running commentaries on everything I do* (or attempt to do, or think about doing..)

Ever listen to a commentary track on a Simpsons or Futurama DVD? Or any Kevin Smith movie? Where 4-12 people are all talking about the same thing from different points of view, sometimes over the top of each other so you can't understand any of them? Yep. That's what it's like in my head. ALL the time. Mm-hmm. Seriously.

Sometimes, when I'm relatively stress-free, it gets quieter in there.   Like they raise their hands and wait their turn to speak.   "They" are all ME. Each one is like a different brain thread working on a million problems at once, then randomly reporting back solutions without regards as to which problem they are supposed to solve. It's a bit abstract... This is why I tend to be extremely habit based and try to avoid change at all costs.   Once a solution is in place, it's best not to disturb it, or the process will have to start over yet again.   As an example, right now I'm thinking , "wow, this is making sense, but who would want to read it?"

"I mean, who would really give a crap? Sure, but as long as we're writing it, it might make us feel better at least. Yes, but then again it could just make me really depressed? Or it could make us happy? I don't know, I suppose the best thing to do is to just keep typing and see where we wind up."

The stuff in quotes there was directly from my brain to the keyboard. That was the thought stream through my brain in the 2-3 seconds it took me to type it.

Read those sentences aloud, then realize that they're stacked upon one another when I hear them, as if 3-4 people are arguing it out inside my eardrums. The longer I think about it, the more of them will show up to chime in on the subject until I break the thread and let my mind wander off onto something else. Rinse and repeat.

The sonic thing is another problem. Actually, sometimes it's great. Makes working on music a LOT easier. When there's too much chaos, I get quickly overloaded - and that frequently leads to meltdown.   I know when it's about to happen, and I try to avoid it or get out of the way -- but it's not always possible, and then I start to freak out in front of people.   My brain convinces me they're all watching, even though I know it's not true.

I start to feel more uncomfortable and begin trying to find an escape route. If the overload continues at this point, I begin frantically searching for a way out and if none is found, I get aggressively angry at anything that crosses my path. Not violent, just angry, like you would be if you were very, very afraid of something. Adrenaline kicks in. It's fight or flight time. It's not *volume* that sets it off. It's when there's too much going on for my brain to process.

If there are 3-4+ people in a room, all talking at the same time, it's like hell to me. This is why I avoid parties – bars -- large gatherings of any sort, actually. My brain attempts to absorb, decode, process, and respond to each and every conversation within earshot. I don't have to be involved in the conversation, just able to *hear* it.

If I'm overhearing bits and pieces of a dozen conversations, my brain works overtime to attempt to fill in the missing pieces and make some sense out of what it's taking in.

On top of this, the ones in my head are all overloaded with input and bitching up a storm at the same time. "Why won't these people shut up? Why can't we just get 2 minutes of silence to clear things up? What the hell is all that NOISE!" Usually, this is when my idiot dogs will start to bark uncontrollably and REALLY set me off. Maximum overload - and it makes me furiously angry at....nothing... for a few minutes.

Sometimes it makes me immediately sad. Not the kind of sad you get from watching a sappy movie or something. The kind of dread that makes your stomach sink down under your feet like you just fell 100 stories in an instant.

Same feeling I get when something awesome is about to happen -- when I'm about to do something I love - when I'm IN love - It's a great feeling, right? I think so -- except I get that SAME feeling when I get pulled over by cops, when I get seriously bad news, when I think about the future. When I think about how much living I've missed out on already, and how much more I'll miss out on as time passes… See where this is going?

I wish I could explain to people the importance of waiting. I have always been a person to take what's available over what's preferred. If I went to the store to buy a VCR, I always knew EXACTLY what I wanted.

The model I wanted was never in stock, but my heart was so set on getting a VCR, that I'd buy whatever piece of crap was available for close to the price of the quality, unavailable model I'd come for. Stereos, games, albums, toys - anything. I HAD to come home with something. This is NOT a good approach to life (or love.)

Since I was 5 years old, I've known exactly what type of girl I wanted. Sure, the description changed a bit as it evolved over the years, but if you take a look back at the girl I had a crush on in kindergarten, she would fit the description of every other girl I ever thought was hot. Tall, thin, long dark hair, not *too* girlie... The face was always the most important bit to me. Gotta have the face or the rest doesn't matter. That, and the voice! The right voice can trigger the happiness center in my brain and make everything seem alright...and I still turn my head anytime I see an amazing set of eyes.

Yeah, I guess I'm a nut because I see eyes and faces before boobs etc, but whatever. There are people into FAR stranger things than I, so no apologies here. What I always meant to avoid were the "Natalie from the Facts of Life type", as that's just not my thing. Yes...I know... I myself was a fat guy – but I worked HARD to overcome that and get where I am now, so again, no excuses here.

I have a friend – that IS his thing....just not mine! Long and thin over short and thick *any* day. It should come as no surprise to anyone that's been paying attention that I wound up with someone completely unlike anything I was looking for.

So much so that my friends and family were surprised I would be with her at all.

I STILL hadn't learned. I looked for the right person for SO long, that I had essentially given up hope. It had gotten to the point where I was worried that I would never get to kiss any girl, let alone manage to get one to have sex with me. I was 24 years old, people.

In today's world, that's practically over the hill, kids are having sex at 10 for christ's sake. At *twenty-four* years old, I told myself it was time to either figure out a way to solve that problem or just put an end to my life.

I've never seriously considered that an option, though. Maybe the first time, I guess, way back whenever that was. Certainly well before I was 24... 14, maybe... The thing is, I realize that no matter how much something sucks, if you're dead, there's NO way to fix it -- there's NOTHING else you can do about anything, EVER! That makes no sense! If you're dead serious about killing yourself over something, you should *at least* try everything possible to fix it first. What else have you got to lose? Being dead isn't going to make anything better, and "better" is the goal. Dead is not a goal, it's the *end* of goals. So, I figured out a way.

I threw out the book of rules I had written for myself and was willing to do whatever it took to get the very next girl who crossed my path. This was after years of trying to get the girls I "wanted" and failing miserably at every turn. I over-thought everything at every step and scared them all away, either by appearing needy, or dorky, or overanxious, or because I was a fat guy, or whatever.

What else could I do? I wanted someone - SO badly – had convinced myself I *needed* someone to complete myself – because sex is such a *huge* thing, right? -- and everything would've been SO perfect with any of them, right?

Surely not, but that's something you have to go through to begin to understand it.   I have never, and likely will never experience a "break-up." It's true. I'm married to the only girl I've ever kissed, so when the fuck was I going to break up with someone?

Think about that for a moment. Give it a moment to fully resonate.   I have kissed exactly ONE person in my entire life. One (1). If this was 1940, I'd be right in line with society.   Yet, it's not, and just about everything in the world serves as a constant reminder.   It gets worse. Being that I've only ever been with this one person, I'm not sure if I would enjoy things more with someone else. I have a feeling that I'm wasting my talents. I have no basis for comparison, if you know what I mean.   With only one experience to judge from, it's impossible to understand something.   I have a feeling I'm way better at this than I'm being allowed to be, goddamn it.   It's like I've thoroughly mastered this video game, but now I need to try multiplayer to truly test my skills. I have this constantly growing need to find out.   To go out and at least TRY these things with someone else. Gee, I wonder what I'm talking about, here....

This is a book, I'm allowed to say "fucking" – or at least "sex". – but yeah – maybe with someone who perhaps I'm naturally attracted to? Without having to force it? Am I *really* asking too much there? To live a fairly basic human moment that almost everyone gets to experience at some point??

With someone who I feel a deep connection with for once….or not! Maybe just remove all sense of emotion from it whatsoever and just break it down to an action, or a bodily function.   Actually, I think that's where it is *now*. Why should I have to do that, anyway? ***Because I made yet another life altering bad decision.***

Truly the stupidest thing I've ever done.   Don't get me wrong. I love my wife in many ways. She's frequently sweet and does all kinds of stuff for me.   She always reminds me how I'm holding her back and ruining her life though.   She's not as good with the kid as I'd hoped she would be, instead choosing to focus on things that let her down in her childhood and ignoring some of the bigger issues.   That's another book altogether.   Now that we seem to know what's wrong with my brain, she seems *less* willing to help me with it than ever.

I'm not *that* difficult to deal with most of the time.   Her job is stressful, I'm sure, but when I've been dealing with a 2 year old and the chatter in my head all day, after getting barely any sleep – and not being able to dream -- for (literally) the 800th consecutive night, I need some quiet, I need slow talking, I need calm. I don't need total chaos, a now-screaming 2 year old who *freaks out* whenever mommy is around, 2 dogs running around me in circles and constantly startling me with insane barking and claw chaos on the wood floors, some asshole setting off a car alarm next door, the phone ringing, and so on.

There truly is no easy solution for this particular problem. In my perfect world, there would be no problem with having a wife and a girlfriend.

Yes, I know, bad me. I don't want a flock of hoes, people… It's just that I get less than half of what I need from my wife. In reality, that translates into "She makes more money than I do." Of course, I have no house payment or bills, but I digress… In fact, she's always complaining about me being needy and clingy or whatever. Right now we're not allowed to say "I love you" because it's "lost its meaning." What the fuck does THAT mean, anyway? And if that's the case, then why the hell CAN'T I have another person who comforts me, and talks with me, and if things are emotional and it feels like the thing to do, why couldn't it go further?

WHY?!?! "Because….that's fucking why." A very wise Norwegian once told me that. It makes a lot of sense. Because I fucked up every decision I've ever made since I was 10 years old. Because my brain refuses to process change. Because I agreed we'd be together forever. Yet, if this were a court of law, I'd swear *she* broke our contract. Her personality changed suddenly - the moment I said "I do." We used to agree on things. Now there was conflict at every turn. Religion has always been a non-issue with me – we wind up arguing about it. Anyone who knows the real me knows what my mind is capable of – she puts me down as frequently as possible for not having gone to college.

Never mind that I went to trade schools, went through apprenticeships, toured the country, won awards, earned titles, taught the subject matter at two different schools, etc. Clearly, not having a college degree has left me retarded and unable to process thoughts beyond a basic Californian 12th grade education.

Even better? Her degree is in something TOTALLY useless in the real world, and while she's reasonably book-smart, she has a total lack of street knowledge, and tends to be totally unaware of what's going on around her at any given time. Her degree that means so much to her is in Drama...and she's totally unaware of her surroundings.... Hello?!? Irony? Are you there? Do you have any idea how hard that is to witness when your brain is as hyper-aware as mine? Fuck me....it's just.....arrghhh!!! -- and then she intentionally screws with me on top of it?? Oh, and did I mention she can't wear her ring because she's "allergic to metals" even though she wears a charm and a watch that would appear to be made of the dread substance. At this point, I'm just going to stop wearing mine outside of the house as well. Fair is fair.

Now, I don't have a problem with the *concept* of being together forever per se. I believed in exactly that for 24 years -- that's what got me into this mess. I *still* don't know how to deal with loss. I want to have someone else *too*. Well, not really. I'd prefer the "right" *individual*. That's not how it happened, so now what?

I have found myself in the unfortunate position of having possibly been "lucky" enough to find a "soul mate" or whatever you want to call it – finally! Yet, years too late to do anything about it.   If nothing else, it's opened my mind up to possibilities.   I mean, WHY is it too late? Is it *really* too late? Couldn't I just... do what feels right and deal with it later? *That's what everyone else does, isn't it?* My brain won't allow it. It'll do something to shut some important system down when I need it.   Won't it?

Either I'll be unable to talk right, or I'll get too nervous to breathe, or worse.   Goddamned brain... Perhaps you begin to feel my confusion? I keep fighting it though.

Even if there is such a person, that would at least *seem* as close to "perfect" as one could hope, I'd never tell her. Even if I thought she felt the same way. *My brain wouldn't be able to do anything.* She'd have to make the first move.   If she is out there, she probably already knows what I'm talking about, and if she doesn't know what I'm talking about then she's not the one, right? Nice sentence structure, and a bit esoteric, but you get the idea.   The brain simply won't allow it to *be* - no matter what - unless proven otherwise. *I think.*

Stay tuned...

So here I sit, yet again, knowing quite what I want, about where to look for it, and wholly unable to do anything about it.

Now I have yet another unfinished thread running through my brain - likely for eternity...like all the others that are still in trapped there. Every time I think of any of them I get that feeling in my stomach again....

Today, I found some pages I wrote a decade ago. The main theme then, as now –

One kiss could set me free, yet the universe mocks me...

10 years – all the experience that can be had in 10 years – and I find myself in exactly the same spot as always. Not moving forward or backward, but running as hard as I can, unaware I'm standing on a giant treadmill until it's far too late.

Every time I go out in public and see people that look happy (especially couples) it fucking kills me inside.

I HATE that feeling!

I'd be so happy if that feeling was to go away, but it only seems to get worse with age. Put me in a room with a happy couple and I'll be trying to wriggle away as soon as I can figure out a way. Except Adam and Samantha! They're happy and it doesn't bother me a bit. Maybe because they're clearly a matched set. Other people though -- the happier they are, the quicker I need to be gone. I understand how ridiculous that is. It's like the most basic, petty form of jealousy.

Why can't I just be happy for others? I've tried SO hard, but my UN-happiness is SO severe, that it just becomes overwhelming and I shut down.

Why do I surround myself with objects? Because I'm trying to fill a void, of course. I can have everything there is to have in the world, but I'll still be sad, lonely, and miserable. Doesn't stop me from trying... Having all that stuff also gives me something to do when things get really bad. I can alphabetize piles of CDs, or sort out stacks of concert DVDs, or whatever. Sorting and stacking is one of the best ways to distract myself, so next time you see piles of crap everywhere, know that I've been going through a rough patch. I put it all away when I'm feeling better.

I'm in the position of being more confident in myself than I've even been -- than I ever will be again. I'm peaking. Eventually, I'll start to get too old, and it won't matter anymore. Maybe I'm too old already. That'd put an end to this little trip right away.

At this exact moment in time, I'm about as good as I'm going to get. I'm essentially in shape. I look good. I stand tall and walk straight. All that nonsense.

I try not to take crap from anyone. I give off an air of confidence, for once -- because I am! -- and it's been great.

Now I'm going to have to sit here again, just like the good ol' days, looking from a distance at someone I would love, that I completely *want* to love -- watching her sitting alone too -- wondering if I have a chance -- knowing I don't for all the reasons that it doesn't make sense – wondering if I do for all the reasons it does -- wondering what difference it makes anyway, considering how screwed the entire situation has become. Each wrong decision snowballing upon the last until it all becomes one glorious mess of fucktitudiness. That's how it goes, y'know?

In the end, she'll be one more person I get to love in silence, never being able to let them all the way in because something or another keeps me from doing so.

It's not that I don't want to!

It's not even that I'm unable.

The rules and regulations of outdated societies that I impose upon myself – the things people might say -- the promises already made and broken– *having to admit to myself that everything I ever told myself was wrong* -- the fear of further screwing everything up – *that's* the bottom line. Goddamned brain… It's too concerned with preserving things the way they are to allow me to find happiness elsewhere. If you listen closely, you can almost hear the sound of "failure…failure…FAILURE!" No, wait, *you* can't…. It's in my head.

All this confusion, all the time -- and that's only one small segment of life... I know I've written these words before. I'll bet that if I dug out more of the stuff I was writing 10 years ago, you'll see a lot of the same things, only at that point I was a *lot* more lost inside. I've learned a lot about myself since then, gained a lot of experience, been through a lot of shit. Yet, the underlying theme remains the same.

I've always been lost, I've just found better ways to cope. Now I'm curious, I have to know...so I grabbed a couple pages from an old letter I wrote to someone but never sent:

"...sometimes I don't understand myself. I have to tell you this – I literally have mild schizophrenia. Don't be afraid. It's not what most people seem to think it is. I don't have multiple personalities, I don't turn into someone else. That's a different disorder. What I have are voices in my head. That's who I turn to first. That's why I don't talk a lot. I have to clear everything I say with them before I can say it. Don't think I'm a weirdo. These aren't actual people. I know this – and no one else has ever spoken to them. They're just my brain's system of keeping me in check."

Almost word for word the same as what I wrote to describe the situation today. For those of you too lazy to look back to page 2, here's the relevant bit:

"The voices were already there, of course. I didn't know they were unique or special though. I always assumed EVERYONE heard that stuff. Let's get this straight right now: I don't HEAR them out loud. I don't SEE things, or imagine things that aren't there. I have no "imaginary friends" (or enemies.) There are *no multiple personalities* involved (that's an entirely different problem from which I thankfully don't suffer.)

That stuff is media driven misconception at it's finest -- made up by Hollywood to more easily explain a non-visual concept. No, what I have are *several running commentaries on everything I do* (or attempt to do, or think about doing..)

All of which goes to show you that I've been dealing with this shit for a *long* time, people. As far back as I have memories (age 2, as close as we can figure) those voices have been steering me – sometimes right, frequently wrong.

You'd think that would make me angry – that I'd want them OUT of there. To me, that makes about as much sense as chopping off a leg because you stubbed your toe. No – this is very much a part of me – that has been there forever and shaped the person I am. Remove that, and I effectively cease to exist.

I tried a couple of the medications that are supposed to fix this. I was more able to be around people, but the *silence* was maddening to the point I was ready to gouge my eardrums just to hear the ringing. That was the end of the medication for me.

At some point I realized it was unusual that I can see myself in my memories. It's like watching old 8mm movies. I can remember things quite vividly - seeing and hearing things as if they happened yesterday. Normally, I understand people would "see" in memories as they would in a first-person video game -- that is, through your own eyes. Yet, while I can look around and see things through my own eyes, I ALSO see myself in the third person, running around doing things on his own.

That may be an important distinction to make. Who is the "me" reliving these memories? Do specific memories trigger specific parts of my brain? *Have I shut chunks of myself off* as "traumatic" events have occurred? I found a picture someone had posted on the internet a while back. I would SWEAR the kid in the picture is me at age 9, but it's not.

When I see that picture, I get confused because it appears to be a lost memory, but it's someone else entirely. That's when I realized I was an external observer in my own memories and dreams – I only knew that wasn't "me" in the picture because I'd never *seen* "me" in that outfit before!

Managing somehow to maintain a first person AND third person view of it all, and jumping back and forth at will between the two (or more?) It's like having to be a director every time I want to call up a thought. Total information overload - once again needing to be sorted through before I can make a move. Plus, some part of me is convinced that there should be a way to physically "step into" the picture and be able to relive those events, and refuses to give up hope.

A time machine would surely make everything all right, but I'd imagine if one was ever going to exist, we'd know about it by now, if only because someone came back to visit. Then again, there are a lot of people sitting in mental wards, convinced they're visitors from the future. What if they really are, and the only reason they're locked up is because we're too stupid to believe them? Who knows... If I knew then, what I know now...

I plan things in advance so that I won't get caught in a frozen moment in front of people. I try to know what I'm going to do each day before I get out of bed. The problem is, I don't usually tell anyone of these plans, so they inevitably get screwed up.

With each additional "ruined" plan, my frustration builds until I can't take it anymore, then I freak out for a few seconds and take off to my hiding place until I can adjust my plans and compensate internally.

When people spontaneously invite me to do things, I always have to make an excuse of some sort because the time required to process that kind of thing is longer than anyone could imagine.

If you want me to do something at 8pm Saturday, I'm going to have to know about it by Friday, *at least*. In fact, the more advance notice I get, the more likely I am to attend a gathering.

It gives me time to think up possible conversations, so I can practice what to say, how to respond, how to act, what to do - so that I won't stumble over my words and make a fool of myself in front of people.

That's why I hate the telephone so much. Anyone who knows me is aware of the need to use text messages. I'm sure it frustrates some, who either don't have or don't use txt, but it's the best way for me to communicate. Short bursts of text containing nothing but the most important 160 characters to get the point across. I can edit, rewrite, add or delete things from my message before I hit send, or can type in all the words required to tell someone off, but have a chance to calm down BEFORE I hit send.

With a telephone, there are no second chances. No take-backs. Once it's out there, it's out there and if I stumble once, it's like a chain reaction. Just the other night, I went through that. In person, no less.

I went to pay someone a compliment, but got too close. I looked them in the eyes and immediately fell to pieces and essentially wound up trying to talk myself out of the hole of insults I'd dug myself into.

Again -- tried to compliment, wound up insulting. It happens all the time. Direct eye contact is a big no-no for me, because I get transfixed for some reason. I always try to avoid looking directly at eyes, which also frustrates the hell out of people. I suppose they think I'm shifty or dishonest or hiding something. It frustrates the hell out of me because I *love* to look at people's eyes, they say so much -- but if I get locked in a gaze, I'm screwed. It's *extremely* hard to function in the real world like this.

Working is ridiculously difficult. The wonderful thing about production is that you can hole up with a core group of people you've preselected and gotten to know.

When I had to work with random walk-in clients, it was always hard for me to not duck out the back door before the session started. I'd have to meet and deal with all these new people every night. That's what finally got me out of the recording school. I couldn't face another class full of new people -- having to make all those excuses as to why the place was in such bad shape - why I had insufficient tools to teach them - excuses for OTHER people. I have enough excuses to come up with for my *own* BS, thank you.

If I've ever looked directly in your eyes and still been able to speak coherently, consider yourself part of an elite group.

I've tried to overcome this. I practice, I consciously make an effort to look people in the eye, but it never gets any easier.

Then there are the image issues. The other night, I walked past the full length mirror in our hallway and did a double take. I saw someone in the mirror who looked a lot like my ideal version of me. Tall, thin, long hair, black shirt and jeans, black boots. I had a moment of "what the hell?" because in my mind, I have not accepted that I could ever look like that. That was how I always WANTED to look when I was growing up. I still see myself somewhere between the kid who was fat for 23 years and whatever it is I actually am. I see a version of myself that is apparently inferior to what others see. I see that I went from 4XL to L when I look at my clothes, but I don't seem to accept what that *must* mean about my body.

Part of this is a defense mechanism. If I think I'm still fat, there's no way any other women would want anything to do with me, so I don't have to go through the inner turmoil that is always caused whenever I get attention from someone. Or worry about the kind of change that would come about if I ever acted out.

It all comes back up - all the times I screwed things up in the past, the fact that there may be a person who's better for me than the one I've got -- but my brain would never allow me to admit that, let alone make a change.

Not without a lot of planning, anyway. That sort of thing would take years to accomplish, if I *could* convince myself to give it a shot.

It's a strange sort of feeling when you start to realize that you have a disconnection between how you see yourself and how you actually appear. If you don't know yourself, how can anyone else ever know you at all? I think this is what makes people freak out and spontaneously shave their heads or something. They're attempting to reconcile their mental image with what they see in the mirror.

Think about that for a second. How would it feel to look in a mirror and not recognize the person looking back at you?

Sometimes you might say something to me that you've said a hundred times before and made me laugh, and this time, I get a different look and get mad at you and shortly go away. If you've spent time with me, you've seen this. That's the physical indication that you've just pissed off one of the voices enough for him to take temporary control and sulk. It IS me – but it might be 6 year old me, or 14 year old me, or any number of other leftover bits of unsatisfied me that are in there.

28 year old me comprehends and deals with things differently than those young, inexperienced guys inside. They handle the immaturity and irrationality. They keep me lurking on the sidelines away from things that may cause or awaken pain. Those things are everywhere, and it's not always possible to predict when the overload may come. I just have to hope for the best and make sure I've scouted the location for a place to hide out well in advance of actually *needing* one.

"The only things in life we regret are the things we wish we would have said, but never had the guts to say - never leave your feelings untold because you never know when it could be too late - follow your heart, it will guide you in the right direction. "

- Anonymous internet person, 2006

Let's get scientific! To begin, here's the root of it all:

Schizophrenia (from the Greek word σχιζοφρένεια, or schizophreneia, meaning "split mind") is a psychiatric diagnosis that describes a mental illness characterized by impairments in the perception or expression of reality, most commonly manifesting as auditory hallucinations, paranoid or bizarre delusions or disorganized speech and thinking in the context of significant social or occupational dysfunction.

That's pretty much it in a nutshell! Impaired perception, altered reality, disorganized thinking, social dysfunction, and auditory hallucinations. Check. Why?

Increased dopaminergic activity in the mesolimbic pathway of the brain is a consistent finding.

In English, there are chemical imbalances in my brain.

Dopamine has many functions in the brain, including important roles in behavior and cognition, motor activity, motivation and reward, sleep, mood, attention, and learning.

That would explain a lot of the lack of desire or motivation I've always had. Like a dog who received a treat every time a bell rang, but wasn't interested in the treat in the first place, so someone kept ringing the bell over and over for attention.

The bizarre sleeping patterns had screwed me time and time again during school years. Not being sleepy until 4-5am, then needing to be up at 6. If left entirely alone, I'd go to sleep just before sunrise – around 7am - and sleep until around 3pm. It used to be so nice...

Dopamine is related to epinephrine, which may explain why I take the sinus pills so frequently. If my brain is misfiring in that department, it's no wonder I have these stupid allergies.

Continuing on:

A person experiencing schizophrenia may demonstrate symptoms such as disorganized thinking, auditory hallucinations, and delusions.

In severe cases, the person may be largely mute, remain motionless in bizarre postures, or exhibit purposeless agitation; these are signs of catatonia.

Social isolation commonly occurs and may be due to a number of factors. Impairment in social cognition is associated with schizophrenia, as are the active symptoms of paranoia from delusions and hallucinations, and the negative symptoms of apathy and avolition. Many people diagnosed with schizophrenia avoid potentially stressful social situations that may exacerbate mental distress.

Yes. I stay home a lot. Alone. In the dark. In "uncomfortable" positions. For hours on end. My feet never stop moving in some way. Ever.

Check this out:

Abnormal enlargement (*hydrocephalus*) of the ventricular system seems to be a common thread.

This means two things; 1) maybe those complications at childbirth really did unlock something normally untapped because 2) there's a *reason* that the information paths in my brain are running at 8X.

My brain is like multiple (leaking) T1 lines where normal people have a dialup connection. An overactive brain with a short circuit in the reward system.

That *does* sound a lot like the kind of person who would excel in school and skip grades until discovering it was all a pointless waste of time and learning to slack – which *also* offered no reward.

That's what causes the multithreading! Because I can... My brain is attempting to function at 110% and it gets confused when it hits the physical bottleneck. My CPU is multithreading so fast and furiously that it's overloading all the subsequent systems! Garbage in, garbage out, right? I can work on all this stuff at once – the problem comes when it's time to sort the results.

I can definitely sense things on a level that many people can not, but have to work that much harder to comprehend it all. That almost certainly spells reduced runtime. *I can burn hotter and brighter, but for a shorter time.*

"When you finish digging up the entire yard, and get all the dirt out of here and we get the pool built, there's a shiny new quarter in it for each of you!"

-   J.A.M., 1990

Chapter 0011: My Maserati does 185

The first time my little mind was aware of the existence of a person called John, I was looking at a broken front door, and an angry set of parents were arguing. I didn't know exactly what was going on (nor are details needed here) but I distinctly remember the words "Why don't you ask your carpenter boyfriend to fix it?" before hearing a car door slam.   All of this before I'd even started Kindergarten...heh.   I tell you this as a reference point.   John came into MY life at the exact moment someone else had gone away.   I still had ALL my learning to do.

I remember playing pinball at Flipper's Bar, where my mom was working to support us, eating Jiffy Pop and just enjoying myself, not really understanding what was going on (again) but realizing that this guy who kinda looked like one of those used car salesman from the TV ads seemed to be driving us home a lot.   He even stopped for McDonalds sometimes, just for me!   Soon after that, the old neighborhood was no longer safe for a single mom and her little guy, so we moved to a (barely) nicer neighborhood.   This guy, who by now I was told to refer to as "Mr. J", seemed to be there most nights.   I'd watch my bit of TV with the two of them, then head off to bed. He even had a dresser in the bedroom for some reason. Whatever happened next must've been entertaining, because by the time we moved to a nicer neighborhood (yet again), he was living there with us full-time.

Didn't bother me any, he was a pretty neat guy, and we always seemed to get along. He'd even started coming to family gatherings.

I remember 1980, when we were living next door to the appliance store, and the kids would always come and ride their bikes around the lot like it was a motocross or something. I, being 6 at the time, was very unhappy that I couldn't go out and join them.

The training bike I had was too small for me, and there was no way we were going to afford something like that at that time. I have no idea where he "acquired" the raw materials, but before I knew it, I was learning about welding safety - wearing a mask and watching him cut these pipes in the garage for some unknown project. I kept watching and listening - he would explain what he was doing (and why) in between verses of whatever the current "4 lyric lines of the week" were.

As I watched (and he sang) I was wondering just what this thing was supposed to be. He assembled it in such a way as to keep it a mystery until the very end, when he pulled a brand new set of yellow MAG wheels out of a box and bolted 'em in.   Pants-Pooping Excitement™ occurred moments later as I was doing laps around the "Price Appliance Speedway" with the neighbor kids until it got dark.

How about the basketball hoop he nailed to the tree for me so we could play together in the yard? This was a man who was not yet married to my mother, hadn't been dating her THAT long, but here he was treating me like a friend - and willingly spending time with me. He introduced me to the concept of checking out boobs via "the Monte Carlo Show", of which I recall nothing, other than the showgirls and their boobs, thank you.

Christmas 1980 was a special one for me. What a houseful! Me and Mom with Mr. J, Nonny and Grandpa, my favorite Uncle Bob and his friend Debbie, assorted cousins running around, old people before they were old and scary - the year of Empire Strikes Back.. I got my AT-AT! Plus some Dukes of Hazzard stuff, and my first cassette player from Grandpa so I could borrow his AC/DC and KISS cassettes. I wasn't too interested in the Bert Kaempfert, but Grandpa like to rock out from time to time, so we could share tapes...

Easter 81 came, we were in a new house yet again, but the gathering at Nonny's house remained the same. Everyone I loved (almost) in one big warm friendly house. Nothing could ever go wrong for me when I was surrounded by such love, humor, and cheer. In essence, the two best holidays of all time for me. That short period of overlap in which we still had Grandpa, yet Debbie and John were in place and becoming a part of the family.

It was but a momentary pocket of bliss. 1981 yanked the floor out from under us. My childlike innocence came to a grinding halt from several directions one rainy November night. Yet when I came home at night, i always felt safe and sound, and I knew that nothing scary was gonna get in past Mr. J. I think Mom felt the same way, as before long, I had an official 'stepfather'. Which was a title he wanted, deserved and earned, rather than refused, as so many would do.

...and while he was not biologically responsible (ie, he wasn't at the scene of the crime...) that didn't stop him from being my father..or my dad.

As one half of the parenting team responsible for getting me here, he went far beyond the normal stepfather. I saw all my friends step parents - they were just sort of "there". Bystanders, not active participants. My friends would come to my house, see how things were there, and proceed to "move in." How much patience did it take to supervise a work crew consisting of Mike, Pat, Ralph, and me? More than a bit, I'd say. All I need to do is mention the words "Line Level" and my mother will start laughing... Mike spent more time there after I moved out than he did before. When your kid's friends continue to come over and spend time helping you out and shooting the shit when your kid is 3000 miles away, that speaks volumes about your character, personality, and accessibility. John was the fill-in father figure for many of my friends.

Some had no father, some had fathers with absolutely no ambition or personality, some had asshole stepfathers, but none had a working family.

Each and every kid that ever spent time in our house - be it over dinner, spending the night, working in the yard for slave wages - everyone got SOMETHING from the experience.   Lives were shaped one little bit at a time. Children learn nothing from yelling and screaming except how to yell and scream.   Make a child laugh - talk to them like they're a human capable of understanding, and genuinely be interested in what they have to say in return, and you do the world a favor.

I don't remember him ever calling me stupid and meaning it.   I *can* recall many occasions on which he told me I was brilliant.

I'm fairly sure he meant it too.   In other words, there was mutual respect, which is quite the rarity between an adult and a 12 year old...or 5 year old for that matter...but I digress..

Somewhere in 1984, assorted circumstances and humorous verbal assaults caused us to relocate to California.   The very first weekend we had together we went on a family trip.   I was generally unhappy about moving away from everything I knew and Mr. J. was trying to cheer me up by scaring the hell out of me. Everything in California seems to be on the side of a cliff.

"Scenic overlook" translates into "you'll crap your pants if you look down" and this boy was used to flatlands.

So we're going up Mt. Diablo in our big ol' pickup truck, and his Spanish/English translator must've kicked in as he started in with "Oooh...Devil Mountain's going to GET YOU!" and generally trying to scare and amuse me. "Watch out for Devil Mountain!" he continued ribbing. I showed him...by going over the edge and tearing my face off.   That'll teach him to kid me! (It's funny now, but I'll just bet he felt HORRIBLE at the time)   It's clear I'll go to any extreme to prove a point....hehe

The next few years would be my teens, and we had the usual conflicts that teens and parents do.   Turn the music down, turn off the tv and go to sleep, take out the garbage, take out the garbage, take out the garbage, take out the garbage (that's what it sounded like to me, and I think that's when I started my "I won't do ANYTHING I'm told to do more than twice because, fuck you, you should be more patient" mode of existence.) but we also had a lot of fun.   Going around to what must've been every single attraction northern California had to offer.

If there was a festival, we were at it, and California liked to have their festivals.   Onion Festival, Asparagus Festival, Wine Festival, Festival of Festival, Uncle Fester Festival, Rocky Mountain Testicle Festival, whatever -- you name it, we went there.

Kept me entertained, gave me lots of time to listen to my walkman and look out the window (essential to any teen) and introduced me to a variety of concepts, sights, sounds, and smells. Those are called "experiences" to those with senses, and I was provided with a steady array. TV time was always comedy time, both on the set and in the living room. We had interactive TV WAY before that was a marketable catchphrase. You can play along at home. Next time Oprah is hosting a special, or Barbara Walters, or Geraldo, or any televangelist, try this:

1. Turn down the sound.

2. Get down on the floor facing AWAY from the tv

3. Adjust level and angle while saying "Periscope Up 3 Degrees, Left 15 Degrees,"

4. Yell "FIRE!" and expel violent flatulence.

I don't care who you are, that's funny right there. That's what Larry the Cable Guy would say, and John would know, as they must've watched that special 100 times if they watched it once. Comedy was always important to John. We watched our share of blow'em-up movies, but the majority of our entertainment choices were humor-based.

John used to like his Bugs Bunny on Saturday morning. A big breakfast and an hour of Bugs would be the last relaxing thing I'd do for the rest of the day, but we always did it together.

In fact, we always did everything together - as a family. None of this "3 people living 3 lives" thing. We all ate dinner together nearly every night, with rare exceptions for union meetings (when mom and I would get pizza) and nights I had to work as a teen. We spent a lot of time together, and they always knew what I was up to (for the most part.) As a result, they trusted me to be responsible. If I screwed something up, I'd either fix it or own up to it (when attempts to fix it didn't work) I don't remember ever being in what most people would consider "serious trouble" I'd get sent to my room (full of music, books, games, movies, comics, toys.....) or something, but by the time dinner came around, it was usually forgotten. Oh, and somewhere in there, we had outgrown the need for Mr. J. and he told me to call him John.

While he liked to use me as a low cost landscaping, painting, and lawn service, I can honestly say I was never treated unfairly. We got mad at each other, sure. I'd go to my room, sulk around a bit and turn my headphones up way too loud, but that's called being a teenager. If you have a teenager or are one yourself, this scenario is familiar. It goes something like this:

"OK, you've been laying around all morning, it's time to get moving. The lawn isn't going to cut itself"

"I wish it would, then you could quit bugging me." (said under breath but loud enough to hear)

"If I quit bugging you, you'd just lay there and vegetate until you're part of the carpet"

"No, I..." Being twelve, this was about as far as I could carry a line of sarcastic backtalk. I hadn't tested nor stretched my limitations yet.

"Enough. Just get out there and do it"

Then, of course, I'd go cut the goddamned lawn (which only took about 25 minutes anyway, once I disassembled our piece of crap lawnmower and poured gas directly into the carb to get it started THEN reassembled it) and would be free to continue whatever leisure activities I wanted to. The lesson? Get your work done properly and ahead of schedule and you can goof off without worry. (and Lawnmower Repair 101) I use that skill in every job I've ever had. Result? I'm the best there is at what I do, though my lack of P.R. keeps me from fortune and glory. This is not only the John legacy, but the family legacy.

We don't seem to be in it for fortune and glory, but for love of the game.

Our entire line is full of people who were/are the best at what they do. Master tradesmen, artists, lifesavers, mothers, fathers, whatever. We ALL excel in our given fields. ALL my parents gave me a desire to *not* be mediocre.

I was encouraged to do my own thing for the most part. I was never seriously denied anything choice-wise. I never asked for an earring (the utmost in 80's rebellion,) but if I had, I'm sure we'd have had a reasonable discussion on the matter before we came to a mutual conclusion. Those mutual conclusions never seemed to be "mutual because my parents said so" as much as they were "mutual because I realized they're correct even though it sucks." Of course, this was before tattoos, piercing, ritual scarring, branding, and whatever else the morons of the future will come up with to be "unique individuals like everyone else" so your mileage may vary.

I showed him though -- All it took was ridiculously bad allergies. My eyes swelled shut and I've never mowed a lawn again. Still, I learned everything I'll need to get MY kid to mow the lawn a few years from now...

When I look at the old water heater sitting next to me and think of what'll be missing when I finally replace it. No singing, no joking, no getting snippy with one another, no stopping for lunch, no annoying mom after lunch, no more trips to the Builders Emporium, no more friendly arguments in the quest of the eventual job well-done.

See, it ALWAYS wound up being done correctly, whatever we attempted.   Sometimes it might take sixteen weeks and involve me running home from school to prop up the collapsing sides of an in-ground pool after a windstorm, or re-digging said pool because the liner fell in and water filled the hole OUTSIDE the liner...but we were swimming in it before too long.

How about the dozens of trips to the U-Pull-It yard to try and fix up my first car? I spent HOURS messing with that muffler and just couldn't get it, then John gets down there and has it fixed in literally 2 minutes flat.   He unscrewed a part that I didn't realize was movable.   It certainly wasn't movable by my 16 year old hand!

John was the strongest human I've ever seen that didn't look like a 'roid monster.   In fact, he didn't really LOOK like he'd be that strong at all - until you saw him hauling steel elevator panels around by hand, or carrying more 50 lb. bags of cement by hand than you could fit in a wheelbarrow.

I don't think John ever listened to an entire song, but he sure learned the hell out of 4 lines, which he would then repeat for about a week.   This was the same reason he could watch a movie 7 times - he'd watch one chunk, change the channel and forget it until next time.   That always left something new for later.   Which is kinda how I felt about John.   There was always something new.

New stories I hadn't heard mixed in with the old stories I could probably recite - New ideas on how to fix stuff that was always breaking at the worst time - new ways to solve problems and deal with life without blowing up at everything (though I forget those lessons from time to time..heh) New ways to distract and disarm your potential enemies with a joke and a smile. The ability to think your way around any problem if you have enough data to work with is not wasted on me - and he knew that, and seemed to encourage it at every turn.

Time passes and it seems as though nothing ever changes, though when you step back you can see the overall effects. The little ones are bigger now, the big ones are older, and new ones are arriving all the time. When it was time for my "new one" to arrive this past summer, my parents were there for me once again. My mom in the delivery room with my wife (where no husband truly belongs..) and John out in the waiting area.

We talked a lot about the present and the future before heading back to the house for a bit. We came back to the hospital and John had to empty out his pockets before we got to the security checkpoint. It takes several minutes for him to dig all the tools, keys, knives, mechanical pencils and other metal based junk from his pockets. He even fished the card out of his wallet that details the metal implants in his body for just such an occasion to show me.

I told him he'd need that ready, as the rent-a-cop doing the security screening was being a jerk that day.

"Being a jerk?" he asked, with a sly grin forming.

We get in, I go through security in one easy move. All clear. John steps up, puts all his metal junk in the container, and walks through the detector.

BUZZZ!

"Sir, could you please empty your pockets and step through again?" He finds some other junk in another pocket and throws it in. Walks through again.

BUZZZ!

"Sir, could you please empty your pockets and step through again?"

"It must be the steel toes in my boots." He replies. The rent a cop gets the wand out and checks his shoes. No buzz. These aren't steel toed boots. Rent a cop is getting a bit concerned at this point. He goes through the gate again and

BUZZZ! Now rent-a-cop is thinking he may have some real trouble here, which is probably a first, being that he's the security screener at the fucking *maternity* area of a hospital, and babies tend to travel unarmed. This goes on for several more rounds until finally, just before the cop is going to enter a complete panic (and hit his little panic button, causing total chaos) -- John slaps his forehead and says,

"Oh! Do you think it could be this?"

...and hands the guy his implant card.

The cop was so relieved he just handed him his container of stuff and said,

"Have a nice day, sir!" as we walked down the hallway together, laughing the whole time, on our way to see my new son - his new grandson.

Just looking around this place will bring back memories - the time we fixed the water pipes, the time we put in the gas lines, all the times you got up on the roof, the years we lived here together when I was little -- every single time I'm laying in bed and open my eyes and see the ceiling you repaired I'm going to remember. The next time I smell barbecue, the next time we fire up a round of Dark Tower, the next time Night Court comes on... I really did learn a lot from you, and we had a lot of good times. I'm going to pass that wealth of knowledge, experience, and attitude down to my kid (though I may excise the section about telling bosses to insert trade tools into their anii, as that has worked for me almost as well as it worked for you, Oh! ..and that bit about using a Veg-O-Matic to slice tomatoes....we'll have none of that either, though the look on mom's face was priceless) Your spirit and ideals will live on through us and him... Ladies and gentlemen, the man who blew the world's first and only Visible Fart™ has left the building. Good luck in the future Grandpa Mr. J Uncle John our good man, I hope you have 1000 channels to choose from on that TV and unlimited Chivas to sip on while you relax in your reclining chair.

I wrote that as a speech for his funeral, though I never delivered it.

hard hard hard hard hard hard hard hard hard life is hard hard hard hard hard life is hard but fun but hard and crazy and just plain hard and sigh etc and no way am i doing that again so fuck you inner child you're not welcome here mr so just go back down in your hole and shut the fuck up so i can get things taken care of and then maybe things will be less crazy but maybe more hard hard hard hard hard hard hard hard poop not digging it at the moment but the morning will start over and progress is made and change is happening and things are weird and happy is sad and good is bad and dark is light and time is fucking evil but stalemate would be a huge step forward from complete and total failure

- 4am thought process, September, 2006

Chapter 0100: Interpersonal Blindness

One summer, we all found ourselves working at Chick-Fil-A. Yes, I know. They don't even have those around here, but too bad. That's where we worked – and they were closed on Sunday, so it was the best fast food job you could hope for. Pat was there first (though for some reason they called him Art,) and managed to get me and Ralph in. Mike had better things to do, so he passed. This was my first job ever. I lied and forged paperwork to get it. You had to be 16 to get a work permit that allowed you to work the closing shift. I wasn't – but all my friends were. Remember, I skipped a grade way way back. So, I got my work permit from the school, went into the library, changed one single digit, and suddenly I was the same age as everyone else. Even back then I knew my way around the system. There's ALWAYS a way around the system. Usually straight up the middle, where no one's looking...

We actually had a lot of fun there. Most everyone knew each other from school, but almost no one had ever hung out together before. There were geeks, rich kids, hot girls, kids from the 'other' high school, etc. Not the kind of people who would typically hang out at school. Kinda like the Breakfast Club, with cockroaches. Anyway, we all got to know each other rather well, and did whatever it was that 16 year olds did to party in 1991. Back then, it meant Nintendo, loud music, and since he'd recently moved to a nicer house, Pat's hot tub.

Truth be told, Pat had become a bit of a dick as of late. He was really into this girl we worked with, but she didn't care, so he wound up dating this other girl we worked with instead, and THEN the first girl was interested.

Funny how that seems to happen, isn't it? So, he went from being a comic geek hanging out in the computer lab to Mr. Emo Fagboy almost overnight and we didn't really know how to deal with that. We still hung out most of the time though, as it hadn't gotten too bad yet.

One Saturday night, he asked me to come over and spend the night because his parents were gone for the weekend. Ralph was coming too, as his mom used to have little problem with him going away for the night, which was always cool. The bad news was that we'd have to be aware of Pat's little sister, who was a gigantic pain in the ass. Not in the usual little sister way. I'm talking about some serious nuttery here. The first time I ever slept over there, I woke up to a huge screaming family mess. They assured me it was no big deal from their point of view, so whatever.

This particular Saturday, he'd invited over Amy, a girl we both knew from years of school, and who'd recently started working with us. She seemed a LOT cooler at work than at school. So did we, I suppose. Yay... I get to take care of this asshole's sister while he tries to nail Amy in the hot tub. This particular evening, Kari – his 14 year old sister - was trying to get drunk.

Ralph and I kept getting the bottles away from her and putting them further out of reach. We weren't drinkers at all, so the parents never seemed to worry about leaving booze around. They didn't have to. None of us ever took even a drop from anyone's house, as far as I know. I got sick of chasing her bitchy ass around after a while, and she was always climbing all over Ralph anyway (much to his dismay) so it was going to have to be his problem.

I took off to the living room, where the big screen TV was blasting Headbangers Ball – The REAL one. I cranked up the Megadeth video and settled my fat ass onto the couch to wait out the evening.

Just about then, the doorbell rings. Pat and Amy are all wet, Ralph is indisposed, I have to answer the fucking thing. I stop what I'm doing and go over there, ready to be mad at whoever it is, since we weren't expecting anyone. Oh! It was Denise. She could stay... I'd thought she was cool from the moment I met her.

I was the guy who trained her in the chicken making biz when she hired on. It was weeks later when I found out she was the daughter of the cool dude who worked at the grocery store. He was always telling me he had a cute daughter, but whatever. I wasn't cute. I think that guy genuinely liked me though, so in retrospect, the following bits might appear much worse.

Denise was kind of a nerd herself. She was quiet spoken, wore glasses, was smart, etc. She was one of those kids from the other high school, so I didn't know her teenager social status, but it never occurred to me she wouldn't be popular.

I thought she was *beautiful*. I never really thought anyone would disagree. I guess my idea of beautiful is just out of whack with popular view. Good! More for me! Oh....wait.... Goddamned brain, you win again!

She wasn't allowed out much after work. For some reason, her dad let her come over once he found out I would be there. Guess he figured she'd be safe with me of all people. Of course, he was right. After an hour of chatting and watching metal videos, she decided she wanted to go see what the others were doing. We go out in the yard and Pat and Amy are being silly in the hot tub, but it was cool for us to be out there. Nothing serious going down. Somehow, I agree, and the four of us wind up soaking in that thing, outside, around midnight, on a hot, sticky California summer night. Wow! Writing that now it seems so obvious. D'Oh! If I knew then, what I know now...

I'm still not sure how it happened, but I remember at some point, Denise wound up on my lap. In the hot tub, wearing swimsuits, with a hot, wet, cute girl giggling on my lap, arms wrapped around me, talking about silly stuff. HOW did I manage to fuck this up?

I never really thought much about it until now. Let's see – and know that if I could go back in time right now and smack myself across the face, I would.

I was too shy to make a move of any sort. Too afraid, as usual. What if her dad found out? What would he think then? Who gives a shit? We have a hot girl on our lap. Shut up and enjoy it. The best I can figure, we were BOTH too nervous to let the other know we were interested.

Or maybe I'm just full of shit and the way it happened *was* the best possible outcome.

All I know is, if I had a wet, hot girl in a swimsuit, on my equally swimsuited lap today, friend or not, she'd know goddamn well I was interested. Trust me. We wound up doing nothing at all. No kissing, no hands-on anything. I have a feeling we were both equally frustrated at that point. It only occurred to me recently though – the idea that she probably wanted the same thing I did at that moment – and also had no idea what to do or say about it.

Goddamned brain – fifteen years is a bit excessive to return an answer to a question, don't you think? I asked myself what to do and FIFTEEN years later, I finally came to a decision. Wow. This isn't good. I can't wait fifteen more years for another answer.

After a while, Pat and Amy disappeared into his parents' room.   Denise hung out a while longer, but soon had to go home.   Ah...her dad DID know a thing or two about teenaged boys. Curfew. Nice.

Ralph had tired of Kari by this time – they'd been chasing each other around the house for an hour or two – she was quick and determined to get that fifth of...whatever!

She locked herself in her room at some point, so we wound up in Pat's bedroom on the other side of the house - playing video games for an hour or two and falling asleep listening to CDs so we wouldn't have to hear what was going on in the other room.   At fifteen, what sucks worse than not doing it? Having to listen as your idiot friends do it.

Fucking high school... I STILL wake up occasionally freaked out because I have to get up and go to school - then I remember I'm an adult and they can go fuck themselves and everything's fine. I almost didn't graduate either -- I skipped 101 days -- FULL days - in my senior year because I just couldn't handle it. With 79 days credit, I needed an entire SEMESTER of credits in 8 weeks. My brain really enjoyed 8 weeks of full time night school, taking such difficult courses as Remedial Reading (I shit you not -- they gave ME remedial reading....we read a book I'd read in 2nd grade - for EIGHT weeks! If that's not the system failing, I don't know what is) and beginning typing (I was speed timing at 135 wpm in the word processing lab I assisted when I did bother showing up...) Whatever.

I got to carry around two fucking sacks of flour that were supposed to be my twin children in a basket for 3 weeks as well. Not degrading at all, when you've already got the problems I had, plus people keep telling everyone you stink and only own one pair of pants and all the rest of the lies - to be carrying two goddamned sacks of pink and blue bundled flour in a basket to and from every class - and I couldn't skip! Grr...

Those fuckers were trying their best to break me, and it wasn't going to work. I had already skipped prom (and any other social event, who the hell was I going to go with?) so it seemed a short jump for me to give them the final 'fuck you' by attending grad practice, saying goodbye to all my friends, then getting on a plane and moving back to Michigan hours later -- never telling anyone I was going-- my friends later told me that I managed to fuck up the ceremony for everyone by causing a hole in the line because they figured I was there and called me anyway. No one ever could tell the difference if I was there or not, and that was the final proof!

My mom went up there an hour later, got pissy with everyone, and got my diploma. Wonder where that thing is? Worthless piece of meaningless shit, to be honest. Everything I learned from school was about survival, I had learned that book stuff on my own, thanks to parents who had me reading at a kindergarten level before age 3. Thank Batman and the Justice League for that, actually, as my dad taught me to read initially by taunting me with his comics. I HAD to know what was going on in those pictures, so I learned what those funny looking marks meant and I was off!

Did you know I can read just as well upside down as right side up? Somewhere around 300 pages an hour, depending on how interesting the material is. I used to "steal" books by going to the store and reading them on the spot. The average paperback of interest to a 15 year old can be read in 25 minutes. It's hard to catch. You'll be reading something, I'll come up from the other side, and be reading right along -- faster than you.   No one seems to think about it when it happens though.

I have some sort of inverse dyslexia. I look at jumbled words, and they appear unscrambled! It used to make John so mad when he'd be watching Wheel of Fortune, and I'd solve the puzzle once the blanks came up, before any letters were added. Impossible!! Nope. Not with the pattern recognition skills I'd honed for over 15 years at that point.

That's how the music works, when it's working. I can sense where the pieces need to go – where things need to sit in the mix, almost as if I'm in the room with the instruments again. When I close my eyes and listen, it just becomes obvious. I don't have to work at it. When it's difficult, there's something unfinished (or not good) about the song – or more frequently, the recording. Mixing is an obvious application for a brain that deals with so many sonic threads on a regular basis. 32 tracks of music are nothing to me – that's like 1-2 tracks per voice! I guess I've never actually counted the voices to see how many different ones there are in there. I don't think I ever could. Some of them come and go. Only a few have been there forever, and most of them are only hurt little kids, or teens – and aren't of much harm to anyone at this point.

If you pay really close attention, most of my mixes attempt to place you in a space – in the room where we recorded – or in my head when I first heard the song. When it comes out sounding how I initially heard it, I win. I'm satisfied. I can let it go.

Otherwise, it's back to work until it lives. That's the main reason I have 4-5 albums of material but no one has ever heard more than 2-3 of my songs in 15 years. You'll hear them when they're done. Any year now...

Chapter 0101: 867-5309

Jennie, you know I could never leave you out! I wonder what took me so long?

The first time I met Jennie, I was 8 years old, she was a little 6 year old girl, and we were in my living room. The very same living room I'm in right now. The story would cross the country and back several times before coming to a rest in 2005 with both of us being married with children. Let's step back a bit.

I was sitting on the floor playing with my trucks when Mr. J's friend Dave came to the door. He was big and scary looking, and he brought some little girl with him. Oh man, how annoying! I'm going to have to stop playing with my stuff and go play with her while she's here. And I did. 8 year old boys consider playing with a 6 year old girl to be top-level punishment. At least they did at *that* time. At least *I* did at that time.

It wasn't so bad, the whole thing only lasted an hour or two, and she was pretty funny. Liked to get me into trouble though! Girls...

Flash forward two years – we've moved across the country to the oddly named town of Antioch, CA. I know absolutely no one, until I realize that Mr. J's friend moved out here too. That may have been what they were talking about so much! Plans to relocate because work was going so badly back in Detroit.

Like it or not, I was going to be spending a lot more time with Jennie.

The initial reintroduction was a bit iffy, but 5 minutes later, we were up to no good together and the adults were well into their drinks, and their cards, and whatever else. We were out of sight and out of mind.

We bonded quite a bit in those early days – mostly because we were all we had. She was my tie back to "home" and I was hers. Eventually, she'd make new friends and stop caring about "home" altogether. I never would – which is why I'm sitting here now.

We spent the night together a lot. We spent tons of time together because our parents would get us together then make her big brother "watch" us while they all went out and did whatever. That was cool. Scott made sure we stayed injury free and didn't break anything. Beyond that, we were on our own. I was 10, she was 8, it was the 80s. What were we going to get into? You have NO idea...and I'm not going to tell you here! We had a lot of fun, grade school style.

I can't count the number of times I'd be playing with soldiers, or looking at records, or reading a book, and look up and

WHOA!

Jennie was standing there naked...again!

If I knew then, what I know now -- I'd still say "ewww..." -- because that was an 8 year old girl! Being 10 (and it being the 80s...) I had no interest in seeing *that*. Mom! Make Jennie put her pants on!

Of course, when we were teens, those pants simply *refused* to come off. Women...

Six months later, after we'd moved to a new city, 45 minutes away, I would begin to care. *Tremendously.* To no avail... We only saw each other on holidays and rare occasions and began to grow apart.

When I was 15, we started to see each other more frequently again. I discovered how much I'd really missed her, and was amazed to notice how pretty she was. I'd never noticed before. She'd always just been...Jennie! A few long conversations and fun times later and I was hooked. Of course, I never told *her* that. I wonder what would have happened...

There's that word again – wonder. At one point, I made up my mind to let her know. When I got to her house to have that discussion, I found her on the couch with her new boyfriend. Took the wind right out of my sails and I never said a word about it. Eventually, I moved away and we said goodbye and that was that.

On our second national tour, in late 1996, we wound up having 2 dates scheduled in northern California - Sacramento and San Francisco.

I would be in the area for about 4 days, and it was always nice to have a place to crash other than the back of the dirty, stripped out, frozen van.   I should give Jennie a call! She's still in Antioch – centered right between the two shows!

We clicked right away – right back into that "old friends" vibe that we used to share.   We talked a bit about what we were up to, caught up with things, talked a bit about the past -- then she told me something I found odd:

She had no memory of several years of her life.

I said something about something we'd done when she was 9 and she said "You *remember* when I was nine?! Oh my god, you *have* to tell me about it!"

For some reason, she'd blocked out a whole chunk of memory.   I have an idea of why, based on personal experience, among other reasons, but that's someone else's book and I would only be hypothesizing.   It's not *anything* as bad as what you're thinking, though.   Just personal.

So I filled her in a bit - told her some of her more embarrassing stories - but I was on a payphone at a truck stop somewhere in the middle of nowhere, slowly heading west and checking in.   I had to go, but I'd be talking to her soon.

We had a lot of phone conversations in the next few days, as I crossed the country and had wacky experiences in town after town. I was certain I'd finally get to have "that" conversation with her. To tell her what I'd always felt, even though it wouldn't matter.

Our lives were entirely different and thousands of miles apart at that point. It *wouldn't* matter, as we never made it to California on that leg. The shows got cancelled for whatever reason, we bailed out on the Nevada show entirely and headed back for Detroit a week or two early.

We were exhausted, frozen, smelly, and broke. It was time for a pitstop. I got to sleep in my own bed for the first time in 3 months, but I'd never get to curl up next to Jennie again.

She got married right around the same time I did. I always felt – deep down - *we'd* wind up married. I love her. I love her family. I love her parents – they spent a lot of time with me when I was young. They were my parents' best friends. It just made sense.

Any time we got close, or were about to maybe – *maybe* – let our lips touch or – whatever...

Something would come up and get in the way. I never had an opportunity. I never made an opportunity. Now she was gone forever.

I'm told her husband is a really good guy. I hope so. I don't imagine she'd waste her time with an asshole. Her mom taught her better than *that*.

Take care of her, Jeff. She means a lot to me. She always has.

Another lost thread - forever afloat in the psychic soup. Another best friend I'd never see again. Another potential lover left untouched. One more person I love who will never know. Unless she's reading this. In which case I'd simply like to tell her:

I miss you, Jennifer Lynn, I always will.

Most of all, to be honest.

(and that's the first anyone's *ever* heard of that...)

For all the things I've shared (and rambled on about) believe me when I tell you I'm still holding back. I've failed on many levels, many times. I'm unwilling to repeat past mistakes, even if I now know how to avoid the pitfalls that caused me to fail in the first place. That would change those "failures" into "learning experiences." In order to fully understand why I must keep my stupid mouth shut today, you'd have to know about the Destiny years.

The day she stomped into the studio, it was like that moment towards the end of Grease – when Sandy shows up in that badass skintight black number and grinds Travolta into the dirt with her shoe. That was Destiny. 150% Attitude, 24 hours a day. I was hooked right away with those type of credentials. The black spandex and Prince gear didn't hurt either. I *was* 17.

Somehow we started talking. I'm still not sure how. Apparently, I summoned up the courage to approach her, though I don't recall the moment. What I do remember was talking to her about Prince bootlegs. I had some cool stuff, but nothing all that hard to find. This was pre-internet. Boots came on vinyl - or on cassettes, crappily dubbed from the same vinyl – and cost a lot more than your average high schooler could afford back then.

She had the Black Album! It was 1993. The album had been shelved back in '87 for being "too dirty" and we had been seeking a copy since.

The most famous bootlegs of this album sounded perfect, being dumped from an official copy that managed to escape before being pulled – but came with a hefty $75 price tag.

A few days later, she came back with a couple of tapes for me. Finally, I had it! And, I had formed a bond with my new Prince buddy, this incredibly cool (and beautiful) girl with the fuck you attitude and the wacked out hair. She radiated pure badass, and I *loves* me some badass! Yes, even still.... Keep that in mind, it may be important.

It was around this time that I started officially working for the school. I'd been working for their studio for a while already. I got pulled out of class one day because a client had walked in and there were no engineers around. Bob didn't want to lose the $80 or whatever, so I was "promoted" on the spot from student to First Engineer. Alone. Trial by Fire! I got thrown into the run down broken room and proceeded to fuck everything up for an hour or two (though the client never noticed) before eventually pulling it all off and "saving the day."

I seem to do a lot of that.

Anyway, there was a built in responsibility that went with that job. Since we were a school owned studio, and students trained in the room several hours a night, the engineers were required to be Lab Assistants. We were unpaid babysitters and narcs – *that's* what we were.

Due to the training methods followed at the time, we weren't allowed to touch anything, only refer to sections of book. At the end of the lab we had to make the students vacuum, clean windows, empty trash, etc and write a report on what they did. Assistants had to write a report as well.

This ate up 4-5 hours a day, 4 days a week – a part time job, entirely unpaid. That should've tipped me off right there!

I wound up assisting 90% of her lab sessions. I remember seeing her name in the book and volunteering to work those nights – extra nights – out of the kindness of my heart and dedication to the school. Yeah, *that* was it. Though it did work out to their advantage. From that point forward, I would be up there 7 days a week, frequently 24-72 hours *straight* – getting paid around $35 a week for the couple hours of paid session work I could pick up – all the rest strictly voluntary. As in, "No bucks!" -- A Bob Dennis trademark.

I was getting a ton of experience, and learning the system inside and out. Without paying them for lab time. I guess we can consider it a work trade and call it even, Bob. You still owe me *thousands* from 2003-5 though, you shady bastard! Though I'm sure most of my money wound up in Jr.'s pocket somehow...

Where were we? Somewhere out there exists a video from one of those early lab sessions. I'm pretty sure it was the same night "Ellis D" set fire to his RID assigned entry level $cientology study manual.   They used to make us ALL go through "study training." I was a high school graduate, I knew how to study just fine. In fact, I had *never* studied a day in my life, because the brain takes care of that. Advantage: Me.   Funny how that course was the very same course you had to take in order to join the Co$.   Didn't matter – we all hated it unilaterally.

When you're paying $5000 for schooling, you don't expect to be sat at a folding table with a bucket of clay and told to make a pencil.   Fuck you *and* your pencil, buddy, I'm outta here! The *only* useful thing that clay ever did was allow Tor to leave giant clay dildoes on Theresa's desk every night.   Also, FYI, scientologists are big on labeling things they don't understand – which according to their own course, would appear to be *every object in the known universe.*

Also in that video appears a very young me. Fresh out of high school, still looking horrible.   Essentially alone in a new environment again, but this time determined not to make the same mistakes again.   I had brand new mistakes to make!

At this point, I had yet to really even talk to any girls outside of Jennie.   *Now*, most of my closest friends are female – have been for at least 10 years, but then?

Totally Clueless Nerd Alert! Damn it, at least I was trying! Besides, she didn't know I was a nerd...yet.

What I didn't know was that she was completely uninterested. Remember, I have very little ability to pick up on things like this. Example: I got in trouble recently because the cute girl at the bookstore was talking to me, and at some point asked me to check out her muscle. I squeezed her arm and made some kind of cutesy remark and noticed I was getting the glance of a thousand daggers from my wacky wife.

Apparently, I was right in the middle of flirting with this girl. I had no idea I was flirting, and I *certainly* didn't think the girl was! Anyone help me out here? Was that girl flirting by doing that?

Given further examples, I guess I'd have to say yes, but at that moment in time, it was the last thing on my mind. It simply doesn't occur to me. I can't even think about how many opportunities I may have missed due to this flaw. It's the single most frustrating thing about my disease. If you want my attention ladies, you pretty much have to stick your tongue down my throat (or at least in my ear...) or I won't know what you have in mind. This seriously limits one's options.

This story apparently refuses to be told, because it keeps forcing me off on tangents!

We continue with our regularly scheduled story, as Destiny was completely uninterested me as anything but a friend, but I couldn't read that. I proceeded to make a complete ass of myself in many, many ways. Throughout a long and complicated chunk of days, we did become friends – then I pushed and pushed on an issue that had been dead on arrival. Eventually, we started to fight and argue, as I was basically acting needy, and she was trying to get away without having to be a total and complete bitch. It didn't work. We devolved into root level hatred at one point, though underneath it all, we still must've cared for each other to some degree, as the story wasn't over yet.

We were working together at that point. The "management" took it upon themselves (or perhaps they were asked) to BAN me from being in the same room as her – *at work*! This wasn't going to work out very well. That went on for a month or so, with me ducking around corners and into studios when she'd walk by.

I bottomed out (and began my brief smoking career) one night while hanging out on my friends session – that she was assisting – with the instructor who used to be my mentor – but who was now spending his nights with her!

And that asshole was married! What kind of fucking asshole gets married and then sleeps with 20 year old girls? Man, all I wanted was one girl – that would be enough for me, for life – and this asshole is doing *that*?

Steve, *I formally and officially apologize to you right here and now.* At 17, I had a lot of living and learning to do. If I knew then, what I know now... I *frequently* realize I've become Steve. Yay.

Eventually, they tired of one another for whatever reason, and she went on about her life. One day, I'd had enough, and I left a letter in her mailbox explaining that I was sorry, and that it was ridiculous for us to not be speaking, and for her to call me if she gave a shit, otherwise I'd leave her alone forever.

She called that night. We talked for hours, then I went over her house and we talked all night.

We've been friends ever since. No further conflicts, no complications. Well, maybe a few. Thinking about the timing, I think I *did* try one more time. Fucking retard! It was a last ditch attempt, at a moment when I was feeling comfortable and emotional. It didn't work, it made me feel worse than ever before.

I *finally* learned a lesson that day, and for that, it was all worth it. I hope she got something out of the deal too.

We don't talk as much now as we used to. We both have families and responsibilities, and we don't get to see each other at work everyday anymore, but we still stay in touch through email and the occasional visit. Hope we will forever...I can't see any reason not to!

For all the pain and suffering we put each other through, we came out relatively unscathed, and a hell of a lot stronger. It's not the kind of thing you can just *understand*. You have to experience it. Sometimes, more than once. At some point, you begin to see the humor in the whole thing. I can see it in others. I watch other people going through the same motions I did. Making the same mistakes. SAYING THE SAME WORDS!

You believe something so fully that no matter what anyone tells you, you simply *can't* change your belief. It's a trap! It really is. You will spend *so much energy* on that one thing that everything else will fall apart. Then, *you* will fall apart.

History repeats, unfortunately. Did I mention the person I'm in love with is in love with someone else? Big deal, eh? It happens. I'm used to it. That's not the interesting bit. No, *that* would be the fact that the guy she loves is also a friend of mine, and has told me many, many times that he just doesn't feel that way about her but doesn't want to hurt anyone etc. Whatever. He could be lying his ass off for all I know. Not my business to dig into. I HAVE to stay out of it. The conflict of interest would be absurd. I can at least trust myself to do what's best for *her*, regardless of what I'm feeling, and the easiest way to do that is to back off the subject whenever possible.

What I see are two things:

1. She's behaving EXACTLY like I did when I was chasing Destiny. That whole "everyone knows what's going on here except YOU" feeling takes *forever* to develop. I'll feel so bad for her if/when it finally hits. Live and learn, hurt and heal. You can always cry on my shoulder...

2. I lose again -- but it doesn't *hurt* the way it used to. Not at all. Now it's just another day. You build up a certain resistance after a while. I mean, it still sucks, but it's not the life ending tragedy it once would have been. It's not like we were *really* going to get together anyway. There's no more fairytale bullshit left in my head. I've seen how that game plays out. When you think that you have everything you'd ever need right there in your arms when you're with that person, it can be impossible to accept that *they* don't feel that way. And usually, because you ARE friends, the other person doesn't know how to proceed without crushing your heart. Hmmm, probably why they call it a crush, eh? Eventually, it all comes crashing down and you get to rebuild from scratch – and get stronger from the learning process -- every time.

I think I'll just take ten paces back and observe. It should be interesting to see from a different perspective. Maybe I'll understand how the people around us felt back in the day. Uh-oh.. Do I really want to know? Probably not, but turning your back on the painful experiences in life is a great way to stunt your growth. Build up that resistance!

Embrace the pain! Absorb it – synthesize it – throw it back at the world as love -- life – energy – beauty – music – *whatever* you've got to give that no one else can, because this is all we've got, people.

At the time, as usual, I wrote a lot to get this stuff out of me. I spent a lot of nights at Eric's house working on this with him while Neil was sleeping in the other room, worn out from running around the living room, 8 year old style.

I apologize for the script format. We were going to try and do this as a TV show because it seemed just that absurd. It seems even more impossible now, but rest assured that very little of what follows is exaggerated for comic effect. VERY little. The names are different, but this is what life was like back at that (unnamed place) I used to work.

Figure out who's who if you can! I'm Al...

Exterior shot, Blue Station Wagon pulling into parking lot. Paul gets out of the car, gets his briefcase, and notices the bum in the dumpster. Bum sees Paul and starts to leave.

PAUL "Oh, don't worry about that. I feel for you. I work here."

Bum walks over and gives Paul a dollar.

BUM "Sorry, that's the best I can do. Get yourself a cup of coffee."

Bum walks down the street to the next dumpster.

Paul walks up to the door. Large sign says ARC/Silver Lining/The Sticks. He fumbles with the door and makes his entrance. Inside, we find Ernie already going about his morning activities.

ERNIE (On Phone) "What the hell are you talking about? We need to have that product, it's very hot product right now. Yeah, I know it's a piece of shit, you know it's a piece of shit, but the little bastards want to hear it. OK, get it over to me as soon as you can."

Ernie hangs up phone and sees Paul

ERNIE "Good morning, Paul."

PAUL "Hey, Ern, how's it going this fine morning?"

ERNIE "Ah these bastards are trying to fuck me again. If I.."

Phone rings, cutting Ernie off

ERNIE "If that's for me, tell em I've already left."

Paul answers the phone

PAUL "The Sticks, ARC...This is a recording studio...I'm sorry, I don't work for the Sticks, call back after 9 and ask for Pam. No, I work for the school. Well, it's in the same building but it's two different companies. OK, bye."

PAUL "Cheer up, Ernie, Pam should be here any minute."

ERNIE "Jesus Christ, that pig...It's my fault she's here. Did I ever tell you how I brought her in here? Now it's too much trouble for her to answer my calls. Lazy bitch, I can't get Ed to get rid of her."

Client from upstairs comes down to leave. Mid 20's, rapper, carrying a piece of equipment.

Paul stands and watches as he fumbles with the door, eventually dropping his piece of gear.

RAPPER "Aw, shit!"

Door swings open, it's Pam. She steps past the rapper's broken piece of gear.

PAM "Looks like you dropped something."

Rapper leaves, looking extremely upset. Pam reeks of perfume, hangs her coat on rack, and sits down at her desk.

PAM "Paul, what time is Fred coming in today?"

PAUL "He should be here around 10, we've got a meeting today."

PAM "(Sigh) Another meeting...I suppose I'll have to cover the phones..."

PAUL "No big deal, it's not like we get many calls anyway. Who was that guy who just walked out? He didn't seem too smart."

PAM "That was Wigwam the Unruly, he's a big rap guy."

PAUL "Really? I thought he was a moron."

Ernie comes in and grabs Paul by the arm. The patented Bertnernie Death Grip . Ernie leads Paul into the hall.

ERNIE "Listen, you missed it last night. Unbelievable. Our lady was on Movietime. Four solid hours. Jeeeesus Christ, have you ever seen a set of tits like that? She's going with our man from KISS you know. Must be the tongue. He keeps the earstraws handy, let me tell you."

Ernie grabs his stuff and leaves

Paul heads towards the back to begin work. As he nears Silver Lining, he can hear the music.

Cheesy rap record with bunch of GC samples. He begins to check the inventory.

Opens drawer, notices 10-15 tapes missing. Studio door opens, Al comes out.

AL, sleepy, "What's up?"

PAUL "How's it going in there?"

AL "The usual. I'm not cleaning today, tell Fred he can go fuck himself."

The clients make their exit, and Al and Paul enter the studio.

There's 50 empty beer bottles, overflowing ashtrays, and an overwhelming smell of Lysol in the air.

AL "Another night at the Silver Lining Nightclub. First they all got drunk, then the console shorted out. What the hell is wrong with Charlie? I've been telling him for a week that this shit was broken. Look at this."

Al gets maintenance log

AL "What is this? 'Unabel to dupli cat' Spelling aside, what the fuck does that mean? Look at this, I can do it for you a thousand times right now."

Al demonstrates problem repeatedly.

AL "He can't fix THAT?"

Hootie walks in, preparing for his Candy Boy job.

HOOTIE "Eh man, whassup?"

AL "How's it going HM Sticky?"

HOOTIE "Awright man, who stole the box of brownies out the back?"

AL "I don't know, been locked up in here all night. Fred was here until 4 am, though."

HM, seriously yet joking, grabbing Al's arm and giving him a stern look

 "Keep your eyes out, man."

Al and Paul go into ARC front office, Hootie comes up front to fill candy machine. The Sticks is having their Monday morning engineer meeting. Floyd and Larry are sitting on the couch, half asleep. Chet and Ed are sitting on another couch. Pam is sitting next to Larry, watching TV.

Everyone has coffee or cigarette. Dylan comes in 10 minutes late. Al and Paul are listening in from the office.

Overheard through wall

ED "We can't keep doing this, man. You guys have to keep your eyes on your clients at all times."

FLOYD "Man, I don't wanna see what they're doing."

LARRY "Right, right, exactly. I mean, c'mon, I had to put a sign on the piano that said 'this is *not* a place for nookie' what are we supposed to do?"

ED "Well, if they weren't a good source of money, we'd kick em out, but..."

FLOYD "Ed, they pissed on your office door!"

PAM "You're so disgusting. Couldn't you show a little more respect?"

ED "It doesn't matter, they promised me it won't happen again."

ALL ENGINEERS "It's happened three times already, and every time they say it won't happen again."

DYLAN "Well actually, the last time I saw em...they said that it was...y'know not a standard thing for them right. I mean uhhh, the one chick that was y'know blowing everyone, uhhhhh That was a liiiiiittle bit uncalled for right, but I mean, she was willing to include me, so I didn't bitch about it right away. {SILENCE} I mean... I just thought that needed to be brought up."

ED "Whatever man. Hootie, how's the inventory?"

HM "Straight. Cept that box of brownies is missing."

PAM "Is Fred in yet?"

ED "OK, I think we've said enough. Meeting's over."

Chet and Tom leave the building. Pam goes back to her desk. Ed goes into his office, Hootie continues filling machine, Dylan gets cast out of conversation between Floyd and Larry and leaves. Floyd and Larry head for the hallway near the coffee pot. Al notices the meeting is over and goes over to Floyd and Larry.

AL "Whats up guys? Sounded like another Monday morning reaming from ol' Ed there."

FLOYD "Yeah. Follicle was in last night. They were charging admission to the session. The 'Some Brother's Attic Nightclub' was in full effect."

LARRY "OH! Dude, Tell him about the piano."

FLOYD "yeah, they had this naaasty ass stripper chick in with them. She was putting on a show for everyone dude. They had her chillin on the couch, right? And this dude walks riight up to her and shoves this dollar bill in her pussy. Shhhtunk! Then they bet Follicle five bucks he wouldn't pull it out with his teeth."

AL "They wandered into my session too. That one chick started getting naked and my clients pretty much slept through it."

FLOYD "They do that. Anyway, later on this other chick shows up and she's going around fuckin everybody, right? Now they started off in the subroom so I didn't care, but they wound up on the piano dude.

FLOYD "I'm tryin to cut vocals, and this bitch is gettin fucked right behind the rapper. Good thing there was a baffle up!"

LARRY "Then they offered to smoke that joint with us. So I'm smoking it, and and I can hear it I can hear it crackling so I'm like hey what's in here?' and Smack tells me it's only a little bit of crack."

AL "Fuck that! What'd you do?"

LARRY "I smoked around it."

AL "No wonder you're so fuckin skinny...fuckin crack addict!"

LARRY "OH Dude! I almost forgot, I had to take apart the console in the middle of the session to clean out leftover 40 oz juice. Fuckin, fuckin beer alllll in the faders, everything's freaking out,"

AL "Not that you could tell the difference"

LARRY " Right right, anyway, everything seems to be working now, so..."

FLOYD " Hey man, got any?"

LARRY "Y'know, I don't, but I'll have some tonight."

FLOYD "Alright man, I'm outta here. I gotta be back in this hellhole at Midnight. Later dudes."

Al and Larry go into Silver Lining and start discussing fucked up equipment.

LARRY "Dude, this room working any better yet?"

AL "Not with Prince Charlie running things. I thought you were going to start doing maintenance."

LARRY "I was, but Fred hasn't had any money to pay me. Besides, I don't want to put in a bunch of dollar store wiring and then have to do it all over again."

Al finishes putting away leftover cords from session. Paul is bitching about having to vacuum up stucco from the control room walls.

PAUL "Coffee's ready! Let's go."

Everyone goes out to coffee area. Billy Rocket and Chuck Coffee come in.

BILLY (to everyone) "Who's got a smoke?"

CHUCK (to no one) "Where's that asshole Pooch? He was supposed to fax me those contracts. Billy, bring me a cup of coffee."

Billy gets two cups of coffee and the cigarette he was looking for and follows Chuck into the back office.

General discussion occurs until the back door opens and Fred comes in with a handful of bags.

FRED "What's happening Sir? How come you guys aren't working?"

AL "Shut up. I've been in the studio all night with the clients from hell."

FRED "You've finished cleaning right? It's very important that the room looks nice for tours."

PAUL "Don't worry about that, we don't have any scheduled."

FRED "You never know when a suck..a prospect might walk in."

AL "What's in the bag, Fred? Hope it's not a bunch of dollar store studio equipment."

FRED "Actually, I got a great deal on these cords. We've got the new $10,000 digital console coming in and I wanted to be ready to install it. Look at this! 500 cords and it only cost me $2.99!"

LARRY "Fred, Fred, y'know, those cords aren't the best for digital signal. You should check out these gold plated cables that Ed bought for upstairs."

FRED "Gold plated? Those cost $3 EACH! No wonder his rates are so high! HA!"

Fred lights cigarette number 2 off the end of cigarette one. Throws butt into coffee cup.

AL "That used to be my coffee, sir."

FRED "Well, get yourself another cup. Only $.25! By the way, where is the coffee fund?"

Hootie comes in at this point.

AL "I used it to get stuff out of the vending machine. You don't pay me enough to eat."

HOOTIE "Speaking of eating, does anyone know who ate a whole fucking box of brownies man?"

FRED "I left around midnight Sir. Never went in the back."

HOOTIE "Awright man, whatever..."

AL "How'd you know he moved the stuff into the back, Sir?"

FRED "HA!"

Fred hacks up his first lung of the day, then picks up cup he just threw butt into and drinks.

FRED "Hmm...not bad. You know what would be great?"

AL "If you fixed the studio and fired Dylan?"

FRED "Besides that. Nicochino! If we could figure out a way to add nicotine to coffee, I would be rich. Paul, see what you can do about this. It's VERY important. Drop everything else and work on this."

PAUL "What about the State license renewal I was supposed to be working on? It was supposed to be "top priority.""

FRED "Don't worry about that. Get this done Sir. I'm going to put it at the top of your list. We can get a license from the dollar store. I saw one in this nice picture frame."

It's almost time for the meeting, Wendy shows up with a bag full of food containers, crumbs on her face and a warm glow.

WENDY "What's happening?"

FRED "Time for our meeting Sir. What'd you bring me for lunch?"

WENDY "Well, I brought the leftovers from dinner, but I got hungry on the way in, so we'll have to order out."

FRED "Are you planning to buy? I only have 38 cents."

WENDY (dumb laugh) "Let's start the meeting. Is everyone here?"

Everyone goes into courseroom for meeting. Fred sits at desk with ashtray and bunch of files in front of him. Wendy sits facing. Al sits down behind Fred. Paul is in the hall gathering files.

FRED "SIR! Bring the file for the monday class with you."

PAUL "It's right in front of you"

FRED "HA! Bring the saturday file then."

AL "It's right here."

FRED "HA! I guess we're all set then."

Paul joins the meeting.

FRED "Let's go over last weeks schedules. Sir, let me see yours."

Al and Paul both look at each other to see if either knew who Fred was talking to, then both gave him their schedules.

FRED "OK. Now, it says here that you were supposed to get our new license. did that get done?"

PAUL "I just talked to you about that!"

FRED "HA! Very good. What didn't you get done from the list."

AL & PAUL "Well, we ignored that and did what had to be done to bring in money."

FRED "So you're saying you haven't done any of this stuff? How much money did we make? HA!"

Silence comes from the both of them.

FRED "Very good. How many sessions were booked this week sir?"

PAUL "Well, I know Guido had an 8 hour session this week, but that was the guy we credited 10 hours for his fucked up session."

FRED "HA! Well, you should've marked up his materials 700%! We're not in the business of losing money, sir."

AL "Could've fooled me..."

WENDY "Be nice. If you followed the Studyology method, we'd have lots of money right now."

AL "If you DIDN'T follow the studyology method we'd have lots of money right now."

WENDY "Whatever"

Wendy starts looking for edibles. Finds pen cap.

FRED "Did the assistants send out the absence and payment letters?"

PAUL "Well, I know Kevin sent them out for the Monday class, but I haven't seen any from Barney."

FRED (slams hand on desk) "Those letters...have got...to get... out sir!" slurps coffee, lights cigarette. "Why didn't Barney get them out?"

WENDY "Well, he had to leave class early."

FRED "Who gave him permission to do that?"

WENDY "Well, he was taking me out to dinner, so I let him go."

FRED "Why wasn't I informed?"

WENDY "I put a letter in your box."

FRED "It's very upsetting to me. I can't believe you went to dinner without me. OK, Mr. Sir, please get the letters out today."

FRED "Where's the outgoing payment file?" Knocks coffee over looking for it

PAUL "It's right there, underneath all that coffee."

FRED "HA!" Starts licking coffee off checks. "They weren't good anyway! It's time to see who gets paid this week. Who's got the straws?"

Ernie pops into the room

ERNIE "Did someone say straws?"

Wendy provides straws.

FRED "OK, everyone draw. Short straw doesn't get a check this week. Cutbacks...HA!"

Billy comes in the room

BILLY "Anyone got a smoke?"

FRED "We're in the middle of an important meeting sir."

BILLY "Well, that's great, but uh...i need a cigarette!"

Paul gives Billy a cigarette

FRED "Back when I was at HoTown, we drew straws for pay every week. I always used to lose, though. HA!"

Everyone draws straws. Fred loses.

FRED "HA! Guess I'll have to borrow cigarettes from you guys all week."

Chuck struts into the room

CHUCK "I just need to use your video machine. Won't take a minute."

Chuck pulls up a chair, dims the lights and begins to view video.

FRED "Sir, what are you doing? We're in a meeting."

CHUCK "Oh, don't worry I'll pay the rental fee. I've got to watch this HoTown tape before my meeting."

FRED "HA! HoTown, eh? Let me help you with that. Do you have a cigarette you weren't planning on smoking?"

Meeting ends when everyone leaves Fred and Chuck to their video.

WENDY "Get to work you guys, I've got to run out for a minute."

Fred comes out of courseroom and enters studio. Al and Paul follow.

FRED "What's happening in here Sir?"

AL "All kinds of shit is broken. Look at this."

Al picks up broken and smoking piece of gear

FRED "That's how they do it in Japan sir. nothing wrong with that. Man, look at all the dust in here. I expect this place to be up to the motherfucker standard. You know what that means this place better be clean as a motherfucker when I come in! HA!"

AL "Then you'd better start cleaning, sir."

FRED "Back when I was at HoTown, this sort of thing was unacceptable. If the studio wasn't clean when I left, I didn't get paid."

PAUL "Fred, you were the janitor, your job was cleaning."

FRED "HA! That's beside the point sir. Back at HoTown..."

Al and Paul head to back office

PAUL "Time to go over lab reports. If I have to hear this fucking song one more time..."

AL "Must be one of Dylan's students, eh?"

PAUL "No, actually, this is the instructor demo mix. I haven't gotten to the students yet."

AL "You'd think he could do a better job on a Stale Bones cover...."

PAUL "I wanna hear this guy's mix. Our first deaf student."

AL "It's gotta sound better than that."

Mix sounds better than Dylan's.

AL "This is starting to suck. Let's fuck with stuff."

PAUL "Isn't it about time for Sunshine to get here? Go fuck with her, I've gotta get these done."

AL "She won't be in for at least an hour. She was out late.."

PAUL "With Dylan? You should hook up the threesome! (laugh)"

AL "you suck (laugh)"

PAUL "Are the fader marks still embedded in her ass?"

AL "Get out of here..."

Guido enters the office

GUIDO "What the fuck are you guys doing? Don't you ever do any work?"

AL "Isn't there a 'one' around here you need to find?"

GUIDO "What? Fuck you."

PAUL "Haven't you gotten over that yet?"

AL "He tried to convince me that his loop was in 5. Rap just doesn't work in five!"

GUIDO "The fuckin thing wasn't working. I got it to work didn't I?"

AL "After you resampled it and got the entire loop, you did."

GUIDO "You can't fade me."

AL "We need to make Bonaduce dolls. You pull the string and it says 'fuck you' 'you can't fade me'."

GUIDO "Yeah yeah whatever. I've got to go buy records. Any sessions booked?"

everyone laughs

GUIDO "I'll check back later."

Hootie walks in

HOOTIE "Eh man, whassup?"

GUIDO "I'm going record shopping. You know that fuckin guy over at Record Land? He tried to charge me $50 for that Brown Eye record that I got at a garage sale for 50 cents."

HOOTIE "I know. whats up with that?"

GUIDO "And then he tried to..."

Al leaves room to go to front office. Paul is on the phone.

Al looks in booking book

AL "Hey, Vince has a session tonight. I've got to stick around for that."

PAM "I've had to answer three calls for you this morning."

AL "We were in a meeting. How would us to answer them. What were the messages?"

PAM "I told them to call back later. I'm trying to work, could you go away?"

Al sits down at desk and begins making drum sounds on it. Wendy comes in with crumbs on her face and a warm glow.

WENDY "What are you doing up here? Aren't you supposed to be working?"

AL "Yeah?"

WENDY "You'd better reach your goal today, or Fred's going to bitch about it."

AL "Yeah?"

WENDY "Well, I have to live with him."

AL "Oh, then it's not important."

WENDY "Just don't sit up here and bother people, OK?"

AL "I never bother anyone..."

WENDY "Yeah ...right...huh huh m huh huh Is my tour here yet?"

AL "They called and cancelled. They found out about the study program."

WENDY "We lose more students that way..."

Sunshine storms in the front door, puts her stuff down and heads toward the coffee.

AL "Morning "

SUNSHINE "Leave me alone, I haven't had my coffee yet."

Al goes back into office to annoy Pam

SUNSHINE (to Pam) "Here we go again. Y'know, I can't believe he expects me to sit here and do all this. Why should i have to answer his phones? Y'know, I'm more useful than that, they think just cause I'm a girl, I can't be an engineer, I'm getting sick of all this."

PAM "Well, you need to do what you have to to..."

phone rings they both look at each other to determine who had to answer it.

SUNSHINE "Silver Lining/ARC Can I help you?"

CALLER "Yeah, can I speak to Porkchop?"

SUNSHINE "What studio is he in?"

CALLER "You don't know Porkchop? He's with George, I need to talk to him. Go find him"

SUNSHINE "There's no one here for George right now."

CALLER "Listen, the motherfucker told me he would be there. Go check, tell him it's important."

SUNSHINE "Hold on." waits thirty seconds "Nope, he's not here"

CALLER "Awright, maybe they're at the other studio. Hey, you've got a pretty voice. Can you sing?"

SUNSHINE "Thank you. (Giggles)."

CALLER "Cuz if you can sing and dance, I'd like to have you over to one of our parties. We always need mo' bitches around here. You can hang with P Nut!"

SUNSHINE "No thanks."

Sunshine hangs up the phone, bitching.

Fred comes up to check on progress

FRED (to Sunshine) "Sir! Are my books done yet?"

SUNSHINE "What books?"

FRED "I told you to get those done before class today. Why aren't they done?"

SUNSHINE "You never told me about that."

FRED "Oh? Well, do something to earn your pay. I'm not paying you to sit here and harass my valuable employees. HA!"

Ed comes into the room

ED (to Fred) "How's it going? Do you know anything about our missing brownies, man?"

FRED "HA! No I left here before they disappeared sir."

ED "Well, someone's taking stuff. Keep your eye out, man."

FRED "Listen, Sir, I've got this great idea, I just need to find an investor."

ED "Oh, really, I've GOT to hear this one..."

FRED "Well, I want to create a designer coffee. It'll have nicotine in it, so you won't have to smoke as much. It'll save lots of time!"

ED "That's a really stupid idea man. Think it'll sell?"

FRED "HA! I take it you want to participate, then?"

Ed walks away shaking his head.

BILLY "Who's got a smoke?"

FRED "SIR! Wouldn't it be great if that coffee had nicotine in it?"

BILLY "That would be cool. Got a smoke?"

FRED "HA! We need to have a meeting sir. "

Billy and Fred head back to Chuck's office. Students begin coming in front door.

Ben Ravage, Mr. Paine, Rick Guile, and Carl Bosen Dorfer are sitting in the lobby

Rick, Ben, and Carl are talking

CARL "Look at that little bitch over there on the TV. You know what I could do with her. All I need is my fucKIN BEer, and I'll be drillin away. I..."

RICK "yeah, I know. I used to fuck a chick that looked just like her. y'know, when I lived in germany?"

BEN "WELL, WHEN I WAS HANGING OUT AT DICK DANGLER'S PLACE, WE USED TO IMPORT CHICKS DAILY. LET ME SHOW YOU THIS TRICK, IT ALWAYS IMPRESSES THEM. GOT A CIGARETTE?"

Ben proceeds to fill spit bubbles with smoke and launch them across the room.

CARL "Listen, that's pretty fuckin sick. Now if you can fill the motherfuckers with beER, THen I'll be impressed. if YOU can fuckin take that fuckin tongue of yours, and do tricks like that, I may have some use for you after all."

everyone laughs, when Reef Burner walks in the door

REEF "Yo, P, wassup!"

PAUL "A two letter word for above!"

REEF "whooooo! You a crazy mothafucka. Is Fred in?"

PAUL "He's in a meeting right now"

REEF "I'll catch him later. Wassup Carl?!"

CARL "I'm trying to have a converSAtion here. If you think you've got something to bring to it, by all means, conTINue to interrupt me. Otherwise, I think you should shut UP and pay attention, oK?"

MR. P "You shouldn't talk about young ladies that way . the kids at my school would be very angry if they heard you saying that."

CARL "I'll tell you what. You bring the little kiddies over here, and I'll fuck the ones I think are cute. They know all about Daddy Carl. 'Who's your DAddy?"

MR. P "Well, I see...hey, take a look at this microphone. I picked it up at the salvation army clearance sale."

RICK "Oh yeah, I used to have one just like that in Germany"

CARL "Microphone? MICrophone? I'll shove your ass so far up into a kick drum...."

Murray comes running into the building, ten minutes after class is scheduled to start. Hangs up his stuff, then comes up in front.

MURRAY "OK, anyone here for Studyology course, roll call.

students bitch and grumble and follow murray into courseroom. Carl lags behind.

FRED (to Carl) "Sir! Aren't you supposed to be in class?"

CARL "Sir! You can't smoke in there."

FRED "Well, that's not a good reason. Put your cigarette out and get in there."

CARL "Let me get this straight..you want ME to put out MY fuCKIN cigarette so I can go learn about some dead guy's study technique, I don't fuckin think SO."

FRED "HA! Got a cigarette you weren't planning on smoking?"

CARL "No, no I plan on smoking every one of these motherfuckers. and they're gonna be GOOD!"

FRED "HA! Very well sir. See me after class."

Carl finishes cigarette, puts it out on floor, then goes into class.

FRED (to Paul and Al) "I've got to run out for a bit Sir. I'm expecting a very important call from Marshall Crock. be sure and get the message.

AL "OK no problem, I'll inform the receptionist."

Al and Paul go up into front office

AL (to Sunshine) Have you seen Partial Cock today?"

SUNSHINE "That's disgusting"

AL "No, really, Fred's looking for him"

PAUL "Fred hasn't seen that guy since the 50's. Oh, YOU mean Marshall Crock...Has she even met Partial Cock?"

AL "I introduced her last week!"

PAM "You guys need to get out of here, we're trying to work."

AL "Whatever you're working on, you need to try harder. I can't imagine ANYthing ever working for you."

PAUL "Yeah, makeup, diets, nothing ever seems to work!"

FRED (from around corner) "HA!"

Fred enters office

FRED "Who's gonna make the coffee, sirs? What do I pay you people for?"

AL "Well, you pay me and Paul to sit around and insult you all day. i'm not sure why you pay anyone else..."

FRED "HA! But seriously, make some coffee."

PAUL "I'm just going to wait until you make it for us. you know you need it more than WE do."

FRED "Speaking of needing it, did I ever tell you about the Fat lady and the telephone?"

AL "No...but I'm sure you will.."

FRED "She's sitting right there, ask her how the story goes. HA!"

Fred leaves to make coffee, Wendy enters with crumbs on her face and a warm glow.

WENDY (to all) "I'm going to order lunch. Anyone want anything?"

FRED "Sir, could you give me a hand over here?"

Al and Fred go into the hallway

AL "Whats up?"

FRED "Well, here's the situation. I've got this cigarette and this lighter, yet I'm not smoking."

AL "And your point?"

FRED "I just bought this lighter, and the damn thing doesn't work!"

Al grabs lighter, flicks child safety switch and lights Fred's cigarette.

AL "Works just fine"

FRED "Thank you sir. how'd you do that?"

AL "I think you need to do a checkout on the lighter instructions."

Al walks away in search of Paul. Everyone is gathered around Wendy's desk preparing the lunch order.

HOOTIE "anybody got two bucks I can borrow?"

PAUL "Don't worry, lunch is on Fred today!"

everyone laughs

PAUL "Oh, that's YESterday's lunch, he hasn't changed his shirt yet. my fault..."

HOOTIE "just get me an order of bread. i've still got those circles for a free one."

Guido walks in with an armful of records

GUIDO "Don't you people ever do any work? All I ever see you do is fuckin eat. I would eat lunch, if you fuckers ever paid me."

HOOTIE "Whatchu got man?"

GUIDO "Don't look through my shit. You've got dirt all over your hands from filling that fuckin machine."

HOOTIE "Damn....whasup with that?"

GUIDO "Fuck you"

FRED (to guido) "Sir, what are you doing bothering my employees?"

GUIDO "In order for them to be employees, they would actually have to do some work. "

FRED "What, you can't fade me HA HA HA HA AHAAA! cough Let me know as soon as you find the one sir!"

GUIDO "I'm going home. Do not page me unless I have a session. Anyone wakes me up for no reason, I put a hit out on their mother, capisch?"

ALL "Eh, fuck you!"

WENDY "We really need to order, I'm starting to get lightheaded."

PAUL "At least something about you would be light."

FRED "HA!"

HOOTIE "Oh shit..."

Lunch arrives everyone sits around office eating. Wendy's tour shows up while she's eating.

WENDY "Eveyone take your lunch in the back, I've got a tour here."

AL "So? they've never seen anyone eat?"

WENDY "That's not the point, it needs to look professional in here."

PAUL "Oh, so you're having someone else give the tour?"

Everyone takes their lunch and heads in back.

HOOTIE "Whasup with that? She owes me change man. Just take advantage of the black man..."

FRED "Sir, did you have a slice of pizza you weren't planning on eating?"

ALL "no..."

FRED "HA! I'll take this one, then."

Fred steals slice of pizza and drops most of it on his shirt.

Class goes on break and Reef comes into office looking for Fred

REEF "Hey Fred, whasup. i been trying to find you ALL day."

FRED "I've been trying to avoid YOU all day sir! HA!"

REEF "You a funny mothafucka Fred. You crack me up. Why'd you send me this drop letter?"

FRED "I didn't send it, it's got Paul's name on it."

REEF "He told me you told him to drop me."

FRED "Have you made a payment recently?"

REEF "I can't afford that right now, F. I been trying to save up for studio!"

FRED "Well, put all that money on class, and worry about studio later. I need to see payments if i'm to keep you on course. It costs money to pay Murray y'know."

REEF "Well fuck all that, I'm just trying to make a record. You need to give me a deal. i can flow, boy. Here, check this out."

Reef begins rapping and the room slowly clears out. everyone heads to the lobby.

CARL "Did I spend $3000 to come and play with fuckin clay I don't think SO. You know what I'm going to do? i'm gonna take a big hunk of that fuckin clay and make a BIG clay cock. I'm gonna put that motherfucker on Wendy's desk and say 'Give this motherfucker a try and call Dr. Carl in the morning.' Then I'll be able to do anything I want to around here. Not that I don't do that now but that's another story let me TELL you about fuckin Japan. i put this chick in a wok and..."

Van Tubroka walks in four hours late

FRED (to Van) "Sir! Can I see you in my office for a minute? Weren't you supposed to be here at 10?"

VAN "Well, y'know, I had to walk in and I live 60 miles away Fred."

FRED "That's no excuse sir. What do I pay you for?"

VAN "If you paid me, i could afford the gas to get here! i had to go to Marshall's last night, I worked seven hours trying to get his console wired."

FRED "That's one of the things we need to talk about. he called me earlier and said it didn't work. Apparently, he pulled it away from the wall to check up on your work and ripped out all the wiring."

VAN "what the fuck?"

Van grumbles and heads off into the back

MURRAY "OK students roll call"

Students file back into class Al and Paul return to coffee area. Carl stops for a cup of coffee before class.

CARL "Just what i need, more fuckin caffeine 'yeah that's what Carl needs' Fuuuuck"

Sunshine walks up to get some coffee

CARL (to sunshine) "Hey, waitress! Pour me some of that first"

AL "just like a woman, she won't do it until you ask nicely..."

SUNSHINE "Assholes..."

AL "We love you too, Bitch darling"

CARL "Where's my fuckin coffee, I need to get in class?"

Sunshine leaves, Al pours Carl a cup of coffee, Wendy walks in with crumbs on her face and a warm glow.

WENDY "I wish I drank coffee, I never have enough money for a drink."

CARL "Well, if you'd stop eating and do some work you might get paid. It's like feeding time at the fuckin zoo in here..."

WENDY "Go to hell"

CARL "Fuck, every woman there probably looks like you thank you very much I'm going back to class."

FRED "Sir! Can I see you in my office for a minute?!"

CARL "Fuckin A right you can..."

Fred and Carl come into the office, where Al and Paul are goofing off and close the door.

FRED "Uh, sir, we can't have you coming in here and upsetting people."

CARL "Me? upset someone?   Who the fuck am I upsetting?"

FRED "We've had complaints from most of the female students."

CARL "ohhhhhhhhh. Wendy bitched, didn't she?"

FRED "HA! I realize she's obnoxious sir..."

AL "and lazy,"

PAUL "and stupid."

FRED "...but you have to deal with it. We're going to have to put you on probation for two weeks. If we don't have any more problems, we'll allow you to keep attending class."

CARL "I knew I shouldn't have paid in full. How come people who make payments never get punished around here?"

AL "If you paid attention in Studyology class, you'd realize that nothing is more important than money."

FRED "That's not true, sir. Pussy's very important too HA!"

PAUL "I didn't know you'd ever tried it."

Murray runs in the room and stands by the desk

FRED "Something I can help you with sir?"

MURRAY "That's OK, I'll wait until you're finished..."

FRED "No, go ahead"

MURRAY "Oh, OK, uh..I've got Reef Burner in the courseroom and we can't find a reference to logarithms"

FRED "Uh....have him clear the word 'log' then clear 'rhythm'."

MURRAY "I see, you think that would help?"

FRED "With Reef you never know. Give it a try and if that doesn't work, send him out to the parking lot to burn one. HA!"

MURRAY "Well, OK, we'll...have to see what happens.."

Murray leaves as Carl lights his fourth cigarette of the meeting

FRED "Where were we, sir?"

CARL "You had your dick about two inches into my ass..."

FRED "HA! Well, do we have an understanding, sir?"

CARL "Yeah, whatever."

FRED "Very well, go back to class now."

CARL "You've wasted so much of my time with your bullShit that I don't have time. I'm gonna go smoke some dope and fuck. Later."

FRED "OK sir, make sure you don't fall behind. I don't want to see any attendance letters with your name on them."

CARL "You won't send me an attendance letter, I haven't missed a payment."

FRED "HA!"

Carl leaves as Wendy comes in with crumbs on her face and a warm glow.

WENDY "Where are you going Carl?"

CARL "Well, like I told Fred, I'm going to smoke dope and fuck. See you later, Grimace!"

WENDY "Whatever..."

FRED "UH...sir? I thought we had an agreement."

Carl closes the door and leaves, laughing.

WENDY "Doesn't look like he got the message."

FRED "Well, I've got to keep him around until that next seminar. He's always good for a few hundred dollars."

Murray comes running in the door

FRED "Uh...Is Reef clear now?"

MURRAY "Well, that's what I wanted to see you about. We started clearing log and he had a misunderstood on the word "A", so we started clearing that, and around the fifth definition, he stood up and said...well, something like 'Fuck this studyology bullshit, I'm gonna go smoke dope with Carl!' I'm not sure what he meant by that, but..."

FRED "Hmm, this is very bad sir. I think Mr. Burner had a blow."

MURRAY "No, Sunshine wasn't even in the room."

FRED "HA! No, we'll have to have him restart the program. At full tuition of course.."

WENDY "Uh...Dad, the state really doesn't like it when you do that."

FRED "That's OK, they wouldn't renew our license anyway."

PAUL "They probably WOULD have, but you told me not to worry about it, remember?"

WENDY "DAD!"

FRED "HA! Uh...I've got some errands to run, I'll be back around five."

AL "Cool, we can goof off for a few hours then?"

FRED "Uh..did you finish assembling those thousand books for tonights class?"

AL "I thought Barney was supposed to do that!"

WENDY "Where IS Barney, anyway?"

On cue, Barney comes in the front door.

BARNEY "Hey buddy, how's it going?"

AL "What's up Barney?"

PAUL "Not his pants..."

FRED "HA! The Barney Tryst smile!"

BARNEY "Oh, that's OK, I'm used to it."

FRED "Mr. Sir! You have a thousand books to assemble. Why are you late?"

BARNEY "I had to wait for my mom to come home and give me money for gas."

FRED "Very well, you'd better get to work sir."

BARNEY "OK, buddy!"

Barney heads for the back, Al follows

AL "How come you were late Barney?"

BARNEY "I just didn't feel like coming in. I was out at Music Cox trying to sell my old Amiger. They wouldn't even take it on consignment though. I guess it's too big of a piece of shit now."

AL "Ask Dylan, he still uses those things."

BARNEY "Speaking of Dylan, I talked to Sue Ellen today!"

AL "Whoa! What's she up to now? Haven't seen her since the day Dylan threw his back out carrying her around the studio."

BARNEY "Oh, she's still going out with Dickey Styles..."

AL "Molester! those guys ruled! Remember their album 'It's Lame'?"

BARNEY "I don't like things that suck, buddy..."

AL "I was interning on those sessions. I remember their producer asking for opinions. i was like 'this fuckin blows! I'm still a student and I can do better' but of course, I couldn't actually say that..."

BARNEY "Dylan Felchboie Productions home of...."

AL "...Molester, "

BARNEY "Dearlord Why,"

AL "and PH Balance!! Strong enough for a man..."

BARNEY "but Dylan likes it too!"

AL "...Well, actually, I just thought...."

BARNEY "Ah well, I'd better make these books before sir gets angry"

AL "Which page are you going to leave out today?"

Barney disappears into the back, and still hasn't pulled his pants up. Al remembers he has to call his guitar player and remind him of their session tonight on phone: Hey..is Yngwie Jr. in?

YNGWIE "Holy Jesus! It's me!"

AL "Hey, what's up, you remember we're in tonight, right?"

YNGWIE "We're ready to rock and roll, eh?"

AL "Everyone should be here...Vince is bringing in his drums.."

YNGWIE "Can you believe THAT fuckin guy? How's our little friend Fred doing? Is he gonna be around tonight?"

AL "Who spilled beer on the console, Sir?"

YNGWIE "and how about Dylan? Think we can get him in there to give us recording tips? What a fuckin genius that guy is...and that fuckin drum sound, eh? Unbelievable!"

AL "We'll have him do the Yngwie solo project if you want...wankers unite!"

YNGWIE "Are you saying I wank? Jeeeesus! I thought you loved it when I 'rock out'."

AL "Anyway, be here around 7, OK?"

YNGWIE "Sure, I gotta go now anyway, the strippers are over and the hot tub's getting cold, eh?"

AL "DON'T FORGET!"

Al hangs up the phone and goes out by the coffee area where he finds Tom Ramsey

TOM "Hey pal! Got a joke for ya! Tell you my latest Fred story?"

AL "..."

Paul walks into the hallway with his jacket on

AL "Paul! What's up?"

PAUL "Dinner break! I get to leave this festering building for an hour. I have to figure out how I'm going to pick up Elvis, eat dinner, and still be back in time for the instructor meeting."

AL "Rock on! Elvis is coming in tonight?"

TOM "Cool pal, I'll get the little guy some sugar and caffeine and we'll go bug Sunshine all night."

AL "It's always cool when he has a battle of wits with Wendy too..."

PAUL "Well, there's kind of an unfair advantage there..."

AL "Of course, he's already made it to the SECOND grade...."

AL, PAUL, TOM "HA!"

Paul leaves, Tom lays down on the couch

ERNIE "Paul...wait a second...(applies death grip, gives Paul a bunch of CD's) tell me what you think of these."

PAUL "Well, it's probably the usual bunch of shit you give me, that even Record Slime won't take in trade!"

ERNIE "Well, you know, most of the product I carry is complete shit. Listen to it and tell me if i should stock it..."

Paul makes it out the door

ERNIE "I'm leaving Pam dear..."

PAM "...."

ERNIE (under his breath) "I can't believe I got that fat bitch a job...."

as Ernie walks out, Albert walks in, looking drunk

AL "Hey! What's up, Punchy?"

ALBERT "Uh..nuthin. Who's the lab student tonight?"

AL "Lab's cancelled. Didn't Fred call and tell you?"

ALBERT "Uh...no"

AL "Well, here's the deal...we're doing in house tonight, so.."

ALBERT "Is Yngwie coming?"

AL "Holy Jesus! Of course he is.."

ALBERT "Will he be bringing....beer?"

AL "Do you really need to ask?"

ALBERT "Cool, I'll come back later then. I'm going to buy some CD's. Later."

As Albert leaves, we see Rollo stumbling up to the door. Al closes the door.

ROLLO (after stumbling to unlock the door) "Ayyy, whassup man, how you doin?"

AL "..."

ROLLO "Awright...is Fred in his office?"

AL "He stepped out for a minute, he'll be back around six."

ROLLO "Aw man...he told me to be here at five for a meeting."

AL "Hmm, I don't know..he said he had some important shit to do, so..."

ROLLO "Is anyone in the Silver Lining?"

AL "Not at the moment, why?"

ROLLO "Well, I got this mix I need to fix up."

AL "Did you bring fuses with you? Cause I have a session tonight and I'd really like to be able to use the speakers."

Rollo laughs

AL (laughing) "Uh, yeah...I'm serious..did you bring your fuses?:"

ROLLO "Naw man, I couldn't find any. But I'll keep the volume real low so nothin fucks up."

AL "OK, first time I hear ear splitting bass coming out of there, I'm shutting you down, dig?"

ROLLO "We Kool and the gang, bro."

Rollo heads into the studio. Sunshine ocmes into the hallway for cup of coffee #30. Al begins pestering.

AL "What's your latest problem?"

SUNSHINE "Leave me alone."

AL "Fine..."

Al walks away and Sunshine follows him into the office

AL "What ARE you doing?? I thought you told me to go away."

SUNSHINE "It's just....everyone here treats me like....I don't know...."

AL "Well, as I've told you several thousand times, you're not going to get much better treatment around here. Number one, you're a chick, and Fred doesn't know how to deal with that."

SUNSHINE "See! That's what I mean. I'm not a chick!"

AL "Could've fooled me....what, do you have a surprise waiting for me in there?"

SUNSHINE "Fuck off. You're just as bad as the rest of them."

AL "Isn't it about time for some stupid reference to a mystical thing that only you understand?"

Sunshine walks away, pouting...

AL "Don't call me too early tonight, I've got a bunch of shit to do."

Rollo comes stumbling out of the studio

ROLLO "Aw man....fuck..."

AL "What's the problem?

ROLLO "I don't know, man....the speakers stopped working."

AL "What?! Didn't I just tell you to take it easy in there? I need that shit to work tonight. I realize it doesn't work normally, but they were working twenty minutes ago, and I'm going to be really pissed if I can't use them later."

ROLLO" Aw, man...I'm sorry dog. I'll go out and get some fuses right away."

Rollo leaves as Al goes into the studio to see what happened.

AL"What a dumbass..."

Al flicks the power switch to the amplifier and everything is fine.

BARNEY "Hey buddy, where's the pages Fred was supposed to update for those books?"

AL "In the usual place...nowhere. He didn't get around to it, you're supposed to use the old fucked up pages instead."

BARNEY "Oh, OK pal...well, I guess I'll sort the files instead."

AL "Barney, aren't those books needed for class tonight? In like, two hours?"

BARNEY "Well, no one ever told me that..."

Van comes out of the back area with a disgusted look on his face.

AL "What'd Charlie do this time?"

VAN "I can't fuckin believe it! I'm working on HIS cords back there, and it's totally dark and shit, right? So i asked him if I could use his lamp. His dollar store piece of shit utility lamp. And the fucking guy totally tells me no. he said that's HIS lamp, and that I should buy my own if I need light back there. What the hell am I supposed to do back there? It's totally pitch black and there's no way I can do anything."

AL "Don't bother telling Fred about it, Charlie's his little buddy. Fuck it, go home early and explain it to Fred tomorrow. "

VAN "Yeah right...I can already hear him...'Sir! How come my cords didn't get finished?' One eye looking at me and the other looking to see who's coming...It's totally like working for Yoda..."

AL "So you just totally tell him 'Sir! Prince Charlie Brown wouldn't lend me his fucking utility light which he wasn't using cause he's a stingy Studyology bastard just like you!'"

VAN "HA! Fuck it, I can't even go home, I've got to go out to fucking Marshall Crock's and wire his shit again. Everytime I'm over there I have to listen to his retarded family fighting upstairs. Still, I wouldn't mind fucking his daughter....I'm gonna go listen to CD's in Fred's office until he gets back..."

BILLY "Hey guys, what's going on in here?"

AL & VAN "...."

BILLY "Anyone got a smoke?"

CHUCK "Y'know, Billy, if you were in Japan, you wouldn't have these problems. People over there fucking worship you. They'd be begging to give you cigarettes!"

BILLY "Well, shit, man, I don't need to go down there, i'm doing a show in town next week, should make enough off that show to buy a whole carton of smokes..."

CHUCK "Time to put on my Porkchop voice and make another phone call...."

Paul and Elvis come walking into the office. Elvis has a backpack full of toys to keep him amused.

ELVIS "Hey Al! Y'know on the thirteenth level of Super Sonic Ninjas...The third guy from the end of the level that shoots fire out of his butt?"

AL "Yeah..."

ELVIS "That guy's cool! But he always beats me...Do you know how to get past him?"

AL "I haven't played that game for a long time. I don't really remember how to beat that guy."

ELVIS "Well, if you remember, could you write it down for me?"

AL "Sure, no problem, I'll try and think about it."

ELVIS "OK, I'm going up front to make some paper airplanes. Daaaad! Can I have some paper to make airplanes with?"

PAUL "Just a minute, Elvis, let me get my coat off first."

ELVIS "Do you think Sunshine would help me?"

AL "Sure...she loves it when you sit at her desk and have her make stuff."

ELVIS "Cool! I'll be up front Dad."

Fred walks back into the office

FRED "Sir, has my client showed up yet?"

AL "Uh...who's your client?"

FRED "Mogwai's coming in to cut track for his new jazz album tonight"

AL "Is he going to massage your belly again?"

FRED "HA! You should try it sometime, sir. It just sucks the stress right out of you."

PAUL "He sucks too?"

AL "Ahead...fudge factor 7!"

Up in the client lounge we see two guys sitting on the couch watching a nature show.

JIM "What the fuck is a tidal wave, anyway?"

JIMMY "Shit dog, tidal wave's'll fuck your shit up! I saw this show the other day, where this tidal wave came down and ate forty six ninjas right off the beach!"

AL "Are you sure that wasn't the Blob?"

JIMMY "Who? Oh, you mean Evil Eye who works here? Naw man, he wasn't even in that show."

JIM "Yeah, but what the fuck IS a tidal wave?"

Fred's client blasts in the lobby

MOGWAI (playing his patented Not A Drum) "Hey, has everyone seen this? It's the first production model. They made me buy it, and it's not as good as the one I made in my basement, and it doesn't have my name on it, but isn't it cool? listen to this!"

Mogwai runs around the building playing his drum for a mostly disinterested audience, disappearing into the back

JIMMY "Who the fuck was that ninja that just blew through here?"

JIM "Fuck dog...did you see what he was wearing? I wonder where he got that..."

FRED "Mogwai! Good to see you made it, sir."

MOGWAI "Are we ready to start, Fred?"

FRED "Well, we're not in until seven, I've got a meeting before the session, so just hang out in the lobby until I'm done."

MOGWAI "Well, before you have your meeting, you should check out this new herbal medicine I've got. You just rub it on your forehead, and hold your breath until you black out. You'll feel so refreshed when you wake up. It's just the greatest thing.....Check this out...I'm popeye the sailor man....."

AL" You'd better breath, Mogwai...I think your brain is starving for oxygen..."

FRED " Don't pass out in the lobby sir. Might upset the students ."

MOGWAI "OK, does anyone want to hear the drum solo I wrote this morning? Here...no....that's not it....hold on..."

FRED "Uh...sir? I think Pam would love to hear you play."

MOGWAI "Great! "

The students begin to file in for class. As we see them coming in, we hear percussion sounds coming from the other room.

TODD: So uh, y'know, tk, what's goin on, <sniff>?

ICE: AY dog. What's the word?

TODD: Yeah, well, y'know, I been going through my book, tk, and I'm hoping we can check out the API cues tonight!

AL: The API cues are shitty! The fuckin things never work.

TODD: Hey, Dylan's been telling me how cool they are, and they really improved his mix."

AL: Those are the EQ's you moron..."

TODD: Tk, yeah, well, OK.

JIMMY: Yo, man, I need some help with this assignment.

ICE: Dang, dog, you aint finished that yet? We been supposed to do that for like three weeks or something.

JIMMY: Yeah, but, I need help with it.

BOB: Here, Jimmy. I'll give you a hand with that.

JIMMY: No, man, I wanna copy his.

BOB: OH..I'm sorry...

FRED (walking in) SIRS! What's happening?

students begin hiding their wallets and preparing excuses.

FRED (walking up to ICE) Sir! Do you have a payment for me today?

ICE: Well, see, this is what happened dog. My mom gave me a check, but I kinda lost it somewhere on the way here. She'll give you a check for double next week.

FRED: Very well sir...(turning to BOB) How about you sir?

BOB: I paid in full, remember?

FRED: HA! Well, you should still give me money each week cause I'm such a cool guy!

BOB (reaching for his checkbook) I'm sorry.

FRED: HA!

Rollo comes out of the studio, looking upset

ROLLO: Aw, man...does anyone know why there's smoke coming out of the speakers?

FRED: Uh, sir? Come with me...

Fred takes Rollo into the office

FRED: Apparently, sir, you've been mixing a bit too loud.

ROLLO: Really? You right, I need to turn it down a little.

FRED: So did you blow up the speakers completely? Vince has a session in an hour.

ROLLO: Really? Oh, I'll go in there and fix em. i just wondered why the flames were there. i can figure out the rest.

FRED: Uh, sir? Leave it alone. I'll have maintenance look at it.

ROLLO: Oh, alright then. I'll see you later

FRED (on intercom) Sir! We need you to fix the speakers in Silver Lining! There's a session at 7.

The assistant, Albert Stale, comes in to set up for class.

FRED: Uh, sir? Check and see if anyone has a payment.

ALBERT: Yeah right, Fred. I'll get right on it.

Albert heads in the other direction towards the back office.

ALBERT (to Al and Paul) What's wrong with that idiot? He's always got one eye on you and one eye on your wallet. God, he came to work today to try and get his program aired, and he "forgot" to bring the check. Cheap bastard's trying to rip off a Christian radio station.

At that point, I stopped working there, and the story came to a temporary halt. It would resume - almost as if no time had passed – five years later. The faces had changed many times since I'd been there last, but the overall atmosphere was the same. Dark, dirty, dingy, and depressing. The boss was still a nutball, there was still no money to be found (or paid with) The entire thing was like a thirty year textbook example of how not to run a business. Like someone's king-sized science project. It's not that much of a stretch to think of those people as hamsters in a cage, running forever towards their scrap of cheese, thinking only of filling their bellies for that moment, and forgetting entirely about the next.

"Look in my crystal ball, its alright
Lay back, evolve, and I'll be alright
look into my crystal ball, its all black
and everybody's frozen in time front to back
controlled by the matrix of mind, body and soul
I'm branded by the system - a carnival freak show"

Chapter 1000: Let's Take a Walk Down the Hallway

Right in the middle of all the chaos and nonsense that was taking place within RID – people being fired for made up reasons, no one getting paid correctly, ownership gone mad – constant recruiting attempts from the scientology people that lurked around there – I knew it was time to find something better.

Eric and I had been working on a compilation CD for the better part of 6 months, and it was looking like we were going to be able to break out on our own. He was working at a production house that was reasonably equipped and closed down completely by 6pm. The brilliant idea was for us to rent the facility from 6p – 6a to run our own productions. After a brief discussion, we got the owners to agree to a reasonable price and we were off and running.

While setting up our gear in the new place, I kept working at RID – partly to keep busy and to get whatever meager funds would be thrown my way, but also to harvest the rest of my clients away from that failing studio and introduce them to my own. It was about that time that fate intervened....

I'm up there one night, around 10pm. In walk the two guys from ICP, complete with about 4 members of their crew. I'm at the front desk, and they knew me from having numerous wacky conversations with them throughout the years.

I'd been involved in almost all of their sessions, in some way or another, so they knew I was "an ok ninja." Cutting to the chase, they had a session scheduled, the engineer had already went home for the day, and there was insufficient gear available in the building even if they HAD an engineer. So, I offered a solution...

45 minutes later, we were at my brand new studio, loading their upcoming major label release into my shitty 4 year old Mac. I was in the right place at the right time. They needed Sound Tools (the ancient form of Pro Tools – look it up..) and I carried a hard drive in my briefcase. What followed were several weeks of editing, editing, and more editing. We finished working on the album the very day we were required to send it out. A stressful situation to the very end, for sure. We all needed a break. A lot of work goes into making an album. This one had been just over a year in the making, as they had gotten to a certain point and restarted once the label deal kicked in. Everyone on the project was just burnt out. We decided the antidote was to make *another* album, as quickly as possible. No going back and fixing mistakes – just doing it like we had to back in the day – basement style!

The Golden Goldies were created on the spot. Whoever was present was thrown into the mix. If you were in the room when we made the beat (a process which took 5 minutes at most) you were required to write lyrics and drop a verse.

Everyone got to pick their own "Gold Persona" – Golden Gram, Gold Rocks, Gold Double B, Golden Warrior, etc. Except me – I got stuck with "Golden Frank" because they couldn't stop laughing at that. Damned clowns....but then, this was still the old, fat, glasses wearing, bad haircut version of me, so I had that coming.

Those of you who know what the Goldies album cover looks like – that's ME! Age 20 – drunk off my ass, cigarette hanging precariously, sweating up a storm trying to fix something in the studio when our little buddy Rold Gold comes in with that fucking camera of his and bang! Possibly the least flattering picture of me ever – gracing the cover of a (bootleg only) cd.

Imagine my surprise a few years ago to find copies selling on eBay (complete with picture, of course) for $50. If you're truly interested, I think 3-4 of the songs I performed on are on my website somewhere...

We made one gigantic, fatal mistake that night. In our state of intense relaxation and giddiness (ok, and intoxication) no one had bothered to gather all the paperwork after the session. Yes, we cleaned up all the spills and messes and garbage and whatever – but we forgot to put away our scripts! So what, right? A production studio with scripts out? Horrible! The problem was with the people we were renting from. To describe them as anal is an insult to the anus. The only thing those people knew was their desire to be "rich", so they kissed all kinds of rich people ass all day long.

From what I understand, one of these rich clients (a self-help person from a "Positivity" group, no less) went into the booth to deliver his positive message and his eyes were drawn to the following message from Satan himself:

"...so step right up – and get a PIE in your fucking FACE, muthafuckaaaaaaaaaaaaaaa!"

Can you believe we would leave something so patently offensive laying around where adults could stumble upon it and be subjected to such filth? Reading this sort of thing could send a person straight to Hell™! Know what they did in response? Unable to "tear up our lease" because we'd only been going for a month or so, they decided to play dirty. The studio was on the 17th floor of an office building in Southfield. Lovely view of the Fox 2 broadcast towers. In order to get to the elevators after 6 pm, you'd have to be buzzed in at the front door and walk past a security guard. This was normally not a problem – until one of them called down and told security that we were potentially up to no good, and should be heavily monitored.

Now, in order for *my* paying clients to get in the building, they had to be put on a list before 5 pm (when I would be nowhere around to do so) AND have photo ID or they wouldn't be allowed in the building. This ruined several plans for several days. The fatal flaw in the system came when they hired a female security guard.

Our problems were over – Violent J smooth talked her into not only letting us into the building at will, but he dated that chick for several weeks until he was tired of banging her. Oops! That made everyone SO mad, they decided to *really* play dirty. It quickly escalated into me pulling all my gear out of there at 3am, shoving the key under the door after I locked up, and not talking to those people at all for the next 3 years.

It didn't matter. I was full time Psychopathic staff at this point anyway. That particular merger made a lot of sense. Psychopathic/Schizophrenic would've looked good on an album cover. Or a police report. It seemed like my best shot at having a good time was to stick close to them, so I did. We went everywhere and did everything together.

A group of geeks in search of something. Primarily, what they did was eat, goof off, and watch wrestling. I was more interested in the naughty rock-n-roll stuff that I knew was going on somewhere.

We had some wild, out of control parties. I've seen things you people wouldn't believe – never *participated* in anything, but I knew what was going on. Somehow, none of this was making me feel any better. Now I'm surrounded by what are essentially groupies – but I still have NO idea how to proceed! I watched as these girls went off with guys far more skuzzy and unattractive than I could ever be.

These were people who had a contest to see how many groupies they could screw before washing themselves... I'd occasionally try to make a move, but the results were always the same. They'd hang out and have a good time with me, then go upstairs with someone else at the end of the night. In retrospect, I believe the problem was with my attitude. I was *asking*...the other guys were **telling**. I wasn't in control – I wasn't confident. I was determined to learn how to play this game.

I spent day after day talking with Violent J about that kind of stuff. He wasn't much to look at either, but managed to do alright with the ladies. Of course, the notoriety/fame helps, but only so much. He explained "the game" to me, told me what he does, how it works. I watched him work his magic many, many times, and sure enough, he was doing what he said he was. Quite an easy trick to pull off if you've got a knack for it. I didn't.

Simply put, I was too nice a guy to even pretend to treat people that way, and that was exactly what these girls weren't looking for. Read *his* book if you want to know more about that. Oh well... There's still plenty of time.

We were just about to head out on our first tour. There had been plenty of shows in Detroit, and lots of funds were raised, but it was time to spread the word to as many new markets as we could manage. When you're an indie label, you don't blanket market to the entire country at once. It doesn't work that way, and even if it did, you wouldn't be able to handle distribution properly.

We were concentrating on a core group of cities – "Clown Towns", as they became known. Cleveland, St. Louis, Toledo, Minneapolis, and Madison, Wisconsin (home to the finest looking women I've ever seen outside of Toronto!) were the first places we would hit.

I decided if I was going to be away from home, I could completely change my look and persona and no one would know the difference. Conformity would suffice. I let 2 Dope shave my head. I got contact lenses and lost the crooked 80s glasses. I grew the little goatee that everyone else in the crew was sporting. In short, I became one of them – out of desire to get laid, quite honestly. Not one of my finest moments. I could *feel* my brain cells dying off! But would it work?

Hell, no, it didn't work! Everyone else in that crew got laid in every city we hit, despite our exclusive diet of 2 Double Quarter Pounder value meals per man per day.

After the gigs, I took care of the gear, or made plans for the next day, or whatever other busy work I could find to keep myself from kicking in the doors and murdering every last one of these motherfuckers. You write enough songs about killing people with an axe, and it eventually becomes a valid possibility. And who would really notice a multiple axe slaying in a rural Florida motel anyway? Kidding aside, what I did *instead* was find my own flock.

It was 1995, so AOL was still a popular way for people to get onto the internet. The web wasn't really functional the way we think of it today. Chat rooms were the thing of the moment. One night, I was online from work, checking emails regarding our tour schedule, when an instant message popped up. Some girl had seen my screen name and assumed I was one of the clowns themselves. I told her the truth and she was happy enough to be talking to someone in the organization. We talked for a long while, and eventually I invited her up to the studio. She showed up a couple nights later (for a non-ICP session) and brought a couple friends with her. So begins the saga of Sarah, Amy, and Denise.

Sarah was the girl from the instant message. She always seemed really sweet on the surface, but there was something bizarre lurking under the surface there. Who am I to complain about that, right? I thought she was cute, we had a lot to talk about, so we began hanging out. Her goofy friends were always there as well. Denise was the little mouthy blonde. She was *very* cool to hang out with, but not "my type of girl", so there I was happy enough when another member of the crew started dating her.

I will always have a ton of respect for that girl, as she got with the nerdy crew guy that she liked, regardless of the fact that Violent J kept making moves on her. She didn't care at ALL. She wasn't impressed by anything he had or any of his bullshit.

Denise and Stefan got married, in fact. Wonder what ever happened to them? The third girl impressed me the most. 5'10, tremendously long dark hair, thin, and cute as a button. Amy was into soccer and basketball and having a good time. She always seemed so unhappy inside, though. Eventually, I'd start calling her "Sporty Spice" (which always pissed her off too much for me to ever stop doing it) This was my kind of girl, but I was hanging out with her friend, so later for that.

One night, I invited the lot of them down to one of our clown parties. I wound up spending the whole night hanging out with Amy as Sarah was too busy trying to fuck Violent J to be bothered with me. It took no time at all to realize I was being used as a way in the door, here, so fuck it. For the next year, Amy and I would be inseparable. We spent virtually every moment possible together. In that one summer, we went to 84 concerts in 91 days!

I have a lot of good memories from that period. So much good music. So many good moments together. The problem was, we were "just friends." Yep, here I am again. We spend all our time together, we share everything, we love doing the same things, we know each other all too well, she sleeps next to me in my bed 5 out of 7 nights, but no kissing – no cuddling – no touching – no fun at all.

Clearly, I was doing something wrong here, but damned if I could figure out what. This was a woman I would gladly spend the rest of my life with, but not like *this*!

Meanwhile, the band was getting more pissed at me by the day. I'd brought in these three women and was trying to keep them to myself. Not true, obviously. What I was trying to do was keep Sarah from being defiled and dumped off like the previous 800+ girls I'd seen him run this game on. I'd spent a couple months trying to get to know her. I had a personal investment, however small. I didn't want to watch her get hurt. I'm not sure if she ever wound up doing anything or not, because soon after that last party, I was let go. They "didn't need me anymore" because the newer, bigger major label was going to staff them up with pros.

Essentially, the staff that had spent so much of their time and energy getting these guys to a point where they could live comfortably, were being thrown out in the cold for their efforts. Whatever. I didn't even try to argue the point. I knew it was time for a change and if this was how it was going to go down, then whatever. I heard a few weeks later that they were pissed at me for not attending the gigs. Why? Like I needed to hear those songs or see that performance again? I'd been through it hundreds of times, and now that they TOLD ME they didn't need me around, I'm supposed to keep attending?

Paid or unpaid, there was no longer any point. The connection had been broken. I couldn't be that guy anymore.

I gave them back any remaining crap I had in my studio and we never tried to contact each other again. I did run into them about a year later. After I'd lost the weight. I was running A/V for the Detroit Music Awards. We somehow pulled the contract to make all the animation and video screens, and they had us running the show live on the spot as well. We were in charge of switching our bits in and out and having things properly cued. At some point, their manager Alex came up to me in the sound booth. Now, if there was anywhere in the world Alex was likely to see me, it was in a sound booth, so this wasn't a stretch. He asked me what time some act was going on, I looked at the stage list and told him, he gave me a funny look, I stood up taller, and he went away. If he recognized me, somewhere in the back of his mind, he never indicated it. I had won again. The new disguise was the finest I'd ever created. I was now hiding in plain sight. People I'd LIVED with for two years couldn't recognize me while having a conversation with me, in a familiar place. Mission accomplished.

"So there you are, come on in, chickie, wow! Ain't you a pretty? I think I'll start with the silicone that's in your titty. I'll pull it out and put it in your forehead and cheek. So now, you look like the elephant bitch freak.

Don't try to run, chickie-poo, I'm just gettin' started I'll beat your head in with a brick until you're half-retarded. Remember that ugly girl you laughed at at the prom? Don't try to laugh now, bitch, you look like her mom!"

Chapter 1001: My Aim is True

The names have been changed to protect the guilty motherfuckers responsible for the following events. This is actually an excerpt from a horror movie I wrote back in 1998, the last time I was fed up enough to write it all down. I wasn't ready to admit to problems with myself yet, so putting all that stuff into "fictional" characters seemed like the way to go. I'll re-read it and make sure, but I don't remember *fictionalizing* much. Sorry again for the script formatting. I'm sure you'll be able to comprehend, no problem. At one point, I'm going to have to edit out whatever horrifically gory murder scene I wrote in there – and the names are false. Otherwise, the story you're going to read next is entirely true.

"Eric" doesn't exist – except in my head, just another "me" in an ensemble cast...

INT BEDROOM

Eric's sleeping again, the phone rings, waking him up.

ERIC (smacking the alarm)

Why is it so hard to get some fucking sleep around here???

Phone rings again

ERIC (answering angrily)

What!

VOICE ON PHONE

Geez, you don't have to take my head off…

Eric recognizes the voice as that of Alison, a former friend.

ERIC

Alison? You've got a lot of nerve, miss. I seem to remember something about "Stop, no, don't"

ALISON

Why do you have to bring up the past? People CAN change, y'know…

ERIC

Yeah, but how many times do you think I'm going to let
you fuck me over?

ALISON

I never fucked you over. It's just...

ERIC (interrupting)

You've got two seconds to tell me what you want before
I hang up on you forever.

ALISON

It's not that easy

ERIC

Nothing with you ever is

ALISON

Look, I didn't mean to hurt you. You knew what was up, and you made your own choices. Anyways, things change.

ERIC

Translation: That motherfucker hit you again?

ALISON

Why do you hate him so much? He's never done anything to..

ERIC (interrupting)

Stop. Your lines are played out. Unless you've got something new to say,

ALISON (interrupting)

I don't know what you want me to do. I called, didn't I? I was thinking...

ERIC

Thinking what? That maybe we could try again? That things could be different this time? What? I'm not buying it again. I know the score. We'll get together, things'll be going great, and you'll start missing Chuck...god only knows why...and you'll disappear. Again.

ALISON

Not this time. He's out of my life. You don't even know... It ended really bad this time, my mom wants him dead and..

ERIC

What about you? What do YOU want?

ALISON

I'm not sure anymore, but I think you're part of the plan.

ERIC

Oh yeah?...what did you have in mind?

ALISON

I've got to go to a party tomorrow night. I was thinking you could take me?

ERIC (hesitantly)

Fuck…I'll go, but this is your last chance, little girl. Fuck up this time and it's forever, got it?

ALISON

I promise I'll be good

ERIC

I'll let ya know. What time's the party?

ALISON

We're supposed to be there by 8.

ERIC

I'll pick you up at 7:30, don't keep me waiting.

ALISON

OK, I'll see you tomorrow, sweetie

ERIC

Yeah. Later

Eric hangs up the phone with an "I've had enough of this shit" look on his face, rolls over and falls back asleep.

FADE TO BLACK – FLASHBACK DREAM SEQUENCE

KNOCKING

EXT HOUSE

We see Eric standing inside a covered porch, junk all over the place. The front door of the house hangs half off its hinges. The door opens

ALISON

Hey babe

ERIC

You ready?

ALISON

Always

They walk to the car. Eric opens her door for her then gets in the car.

INT CAR [17]

The music's playing, they drive along for several minutes without a word.

ERIC

Why is it that you don't speak when you're in a car? Any other time I can't shut you up.

ALISON

I don't know, I just kinda space out.

ERIC

Maybe if you learned to drive it'd take some of the mystery out of it.

Eric turns the radio up for the duration of the ride. Not another word is spoken.

The car drives down the road

CUT TO INT HOUSE [18]

We see Eric and Alison entering the party. The house is filled with Alison's friends. Eric feels immediately out of place.

STONER DUDE

Hey Ali!

ALISON

Hey Jason, what's up babe? This is Eric.

JASON (to Eric)

Nice to meet you. Drinks in the kitchen, good stuff's over here.

ERIC

Cool.

Ali heads into the kitchen to get a drink. There's nowhere to sit.

Eric grabs a spot on the living room floor with 5 or 6 wasted people around him. He notices Ali's friend Melissa sitting across the room and heads over to talk with her.

INT KITCHEN

Ali gets her drink and sits down at the table with Jason and two other guys. We see Eric looking from the other room. Ali waves him to come in the kitchen.

ERIC (entering kitchen)

What's up?

ALISON

Everybody, this is Eric.

EVERYBODY

Hey

Eric nods his head in recognition. He sees one of the guys rolling a joint.

STONER 1

You're just in time guys.

Stoner 1 lights the joint, hits it, and passes it to Ali.

STONER 3

So, Eric, how long you known Ali?

ERIC

Bout a year, on and off

STONER 3

Whoa! How come we've never met you before?

ALI (exhaling)

It's a long story that we don't need to get into right now, dahlink

Ali passes the joint to Eric, who takes a quick hit and passes it to Jason

ERIC

Whatever she says...

The joint passes around the table, everyone is adlibbing again, general getting to know someone conversation.

STONER 2

Ali, where's Chuck been? Haven't seen him around.

ALISON

Don't know, don't care

STONER 2

Gotcha...

Jason pulls a small vial out of his pocket, dumps the contents on a plate, and begins separating it into small lines.

STONER 2

Shit, Jason. You been holding out on me, bro?

Jason snorts a couple lines of coke, Then passes the plate to stoner 2, who also snorts.

JASON (offering)

Eric?

ERIC

Um... No. Thanks.

Eric doesn't want any part of this and starts heading back into the living room to find Melissa. [19]

JASON

How bout you, Ali?

ALI

No, I'd better not.

Eric feels relieved. He knew she wouldn't go there.

JASON

C'mon, just a couple?

ALISON

Well...you talked me into it.

Alison takes the plate and does a couple lines. Eric watches and you can see the blood drain from his face as if the world had fallen out from underneath him. He heads towards the bathroom, almost knocking Melissa over. [20]

MELISSA

What's up Eric?

Eric doesn't respond. He doesn't have time. As soon as he gets in the bathroom he pukes, rinses his mouth out, sits down on the toilet and lights a smoke. A strange look crosses his face. A few minutes pass and a knock comes at the door.

MELISSA (through door)

Eric? You OK?

ERIC

Yeah...I'll be out in a minute.

Eric comes out of the bathroom

MELISSA

Eric? What's going on?

Eric walks past Melissa over to Ali.

ERIC

I just remembered I've got to be somewhere else.

ALISON

Now? We just got here.

ERIC

It's important. I've GOT to go.

ALISON (disappointed)

OK. Call me tomorrow?

ERIC (with a look of disbelief)

Yeah...yeah sure. Later everybody.

EVERYBODY

Take it easy

Eric turns and walks out the door, not looking back. Obviously stunned by what has just happened. We see him slowly walking to his car, head hung low. He gets in the car.

INT CAR

Eric punches the steering wheel, starts the car and pulls off fast. He turns on the radio. Eric screams in anger. He pops the tape out of the deck and throws it out the window. He pops in another tape. Eric drives home, way too fast, super pissed and jamming along.

ERIC'S POV

Looking through Eric's eyes, we see him get out of the car, slam through the front door, and kick open his bedroom door.

NORMAL VIEW

We see Eric having a fit. He's breaking everything he can get ahold of, as a release for the anger that's built up inside of him. He grabs a baseball bat and goes for the stereo. He can't bring himself to do it. He begins to calm down and instead of destroying his stereo, he turns it on.

ERIC

Not a good idea, Eric... Don't smash the one thing that keeps you happy.

The song on the radio changes and sparks an old memory. The wrong memory. The look in Eric's eyes is pure death, with a pinch of hurt and fear mixed in for flavor.

He turns and smashes his speakers, one at a time before directing his anger towards the stereo. Over and over we see him hit it with the bat until there's nothing but little chunks of plastic and metal.

FADE TO BLACK

FADE IN - INT BEDROOM

Eric wakes up, safe in his bed. He starts to get ready for his date.

FADE TO BLACK

KNOCKING

EXT HOUSE

We see Eric standing inside a covered porch, waiting. The door opens.

ALISON

Hey babe

ERIC

You ready?

ALISON

Always!

They walk to the car. Eric opens her door for her then gets in the car.

INT CAR ²⁴

The music's playing, they drive along for several minutes without a word.

ERIC

Here we go again...

They pull up in front of an old brick house. We see Eric open her door for her, then they walk up the steps and into the house.

ALISON (leading Eric by the hand)

We have arrived

ROSE

Merry Christmas Ali. Good to see you again Eric.

ERIC

Yep, I'm still around...amazing, eh?

The distance from the front door to the table is about 2 feet. Eric and Ali sit down and get comfortable. Rose brings them both a beer

ERIC

Oh..no thanks, I brought some pop...I know I'll be the one driving home tonight.

ROSE (taking the beer for herself)

OK...they're in there if you want 'em. Do you need a glass

ERIC

No...I'm all set

Meanwhile, in the time it took for that little dialogue, Ali finished her first beer and heads into the kitchen.

STEVE

Hey Eric! Bring me any weed?

ERIC (amazed at Steve's obvious ignorance)

Huh?

STEVE

It's cool, man.

ERIC (shaking off his stun)

No. No, I didn't bring any weed

Ali comes back in the dining room and sits down almost on Eric's lap, beer in hand.

ALISON

What'd I miss, babe?

ERIC

The usual bunch of nothing. We were sharing a moment

ALISON (eyebrow cocked)

Oh, reALLy?

Ali sits ON Eric's lap and wraps her arms around him.

ALISON

Don't you prefer your warm moments WITH me?

ERIC (trying to conceal his growing amazement)

2 to 1 over the leading cat food

ALISON

Oh, you love me...

ERIC

You wouldn't pass the initiation

ALISON

What initiation?

ERIC(laughing)

If you have to ask, you'd never pass.

ALISON

I'm really going to teach you a lesson tonight.

ERIC (blushing)

Uhm...yeah, right...So, Steve, you bring me any weed?

STEVE

Hey, no man. Did you?

FADE TO BLACK

Scene fades back in a bit later

ERIC (motioning to TV)

...I mean, look at this. Right there, how old is that chick? 15! THAT is what 15 year old girls look like these days. What's happening? Pretty soon they're going to have to make you an adult at 10.

ALI

Yeah, but will she ever be able to do this?

Ali clacks her tongue piercing against her front teeth and slaps Eric playfully

ALI

Guaranteed I can make you appreciate it.

ERIC

Oh, I'm sure you can.   That's not the point at all!

Beer bottles are everywhere

ERIC (whispering)

Ali, that's six. Don't get too fucked up, I've got plans for you.

ALI (already drunk)

Just one more babe. Then we'll get out of here.

BETH

So, Ali, do you have a special present for Eric tonight?

ALI

Never know. This is my baby. See, you guys don't know.
He's just the sweetest guy in the entire world.

ERIC

Let's not discuss my taste in public.

ALI

Do you know what he gave me today? Check this out.

She pulls a piece of paper from her purse. Eric looks like he wants to disappear.

ALI (reading)

"Always watching as you make your every move"

"Love is such a silly game to you"

"I lay here watching you breathe"

"Still I know I can't contain you..."

We cut away back from our horror movie sequence to see Ali putting the paper back into her purse. He'd written her a poem in which the first letter of each sentence spelled out her entire name. First, middle and last.

ROSE (putting her arm around Eric)

Don't let go of this one Ali. I'll have to grab him for myself.

Ali comes back in with another beer. She can hardly walk at this point.

She sits on Eric's lap again.

ALI

Sorry girls. This one's all mine.

ALI (whispering to Eric)

Lemme finish this beer and we'll leave. They've convinced me I need to hang on to you. So when we get home, I'm going to give you anything you want. You're the only man I'll ever need. You know? Cause you accept me as I am, you never try to make me into someone else.

ERIC

I don't WANT someone else.

ALI

That's why I love you.

ALI (kissing him)

Say it

ERIC

It.

ALI

Tell me you love me

ERIC

I love you, Alison Lee Smith. Do I get to unwrap my presents this time?

ALI

You'll have a *very* merry christmas.

ERIC (grinning)

Drink up.

ERIC (returning to the conversation)

So, what are we talking about?

ALI

I'll be right back and then we can go.

Ali stumbles off to the bathroom

ROSE

I think it's so sweet of you to not drink tonight. It's nice to know she'll make it home alive for a change.

ERIC

Yeah, well, I'm pretty harmless

Suddenly we hear a loud crash

ROSE

Ali? You OK?

No response from the bathroom. Rose gets up and goes in there.

Rose leads Ali from the bathroom. Ali's got her dress tucked into her pantyhose, there's a bit of puke dribbling down the front of her. They go into the bedroom. Eric goes in there in time to see Ali fall face down on the wooden floor.

ERIC

Wow! Now there's something I've never seen before!

ROSE

I think someone's had a few too many. Can you take care of her for me?

ERIC

Yeah. Go do what you've got to do. I'll deal with this.

ROSE

Thanks sweetie. There's pillows and blankets and stuff in the closet.

Rose heads out to clean up the mess in the bathroom. Eric moves Ali onto the bed and takes off her shoes.

ERIC

If I could have bet money...

The window is cracked and the room is about 15 degrees. He takes off his shoes and climbs into bed next to Ali. He props her head up to prevent Bon Scott syndrome and wipes some drool off her chin. He's watching her sleep and holding her almost as if she were a child. Eric, eager for the day to end dozes off as well.

FADE IN - BEDROOM MORNING

ALI

Wow...how many beers did I drink

ERIC (waking up)

That would be 13.

ALI

I thought you were going to stop me after 6.

ERIC

I tried to stop you after 6, 7, 8, and 9. You weren't listening to me...

ALI

Oh my god...What time is it?

ERIC

Somewhere round 7

ALI

We've got to go!

Ali starts fixing herself up.

ERIC

I wouldn't worry too much about that.

ALI

Yeah, but it's Christmas morning. Joy... Get up and get ready. I'm going to pee and we're leaving.

ERIC

Try not to fall down this time

ALI

Huh? What are you talking about?

ERIC

You don't remember? You fell down in the bathroom last night? Puke on your dress? You tucked your dress into your pantyhose? Any of this sound familiar?

ALI

The last thing I remember was watching something on TV

ERIC

Really...you missed all the best parts!

ALI

Get ready.

She walks out the door and heads to the bathroom. Eric gets up and runs a comb through his hair. He pulls out a cigarette and lights it.

ERIC

Fuck fried eggs. That bitch's brain is *hard boiled*.

CUT TO EXT HOUSE

We see them getting into Eric's car.

INT CAR.

Eric starts the car. The radio's on already. He goes to turn on the heat.

ERIC

Jesus Christ! What next!

ALI
What's the problem?

ERIC
Now the fucking heat doesn't work. I should've known. Fucking thing wouldn't turn off all summer long. Now that it's cold, why would it work?

He turns up the radio and drives off.

CUT TO EXT HOUSE

We see Eric's car pull up in Ali's driveway

ERIC

There ya go. Another Merry fucking Christmas...

Note: the following is NOT a true story, but was what my brain decided might fill in the blank in the story at the time. Wishful thinking, so to speak.   Odd to read it back now, knowing what I do now... Grrr!!!

FADE TO BLACK

Eric suddenly wakes up, picks up the phone, and dials.

FEMALE VOICE

Hello?

ERIC

Hi! You don't know me, but let me start off by saying this is not a salespitch. Nor is it a prank of any sort.

VOICE

Hmmm...sounds interesting.

ERIC

Cool. This may seem like an odd question, but how old are you?

VOICE

This doesn't sound like your average pervert fare.

ERIC

I told you, I'm not a pervert. It's a long story, but I'm looking for a single girl in her early 20's and I'm thinking she's there. By any chance is she you?

VOICE

Could be, I fit your description, anyway. Who is this?

ERIC

It doesn't matter yet. We need to get to know each other first.

VOICE

Do you understand how weird I would have to be to keep talking to you?

ERIC

You'd have to be at LEAST that weird for me to WANT to talk to you...

VOICE

I see....sooooo, what do you like?

ERIC

Hey! Who's the weirdo here? Me first. Tell me about yourself, what you do, what you'd like to do, etc.

VOICE

God, I can't believe I'm doing this... OK, should we start with looks? I'm...

ERIC (interrupting)

Nonono...hold on, I said "tell me about yourself" not, "describe yourself."

I don't care what you look like because, quite frankly, anything you say over the phone to a complete stranger may not be exactly accurate, y'know?

VOICE

Well, what then?

ERIC

What do you do for fun, girlie?

VOICE

Y'know, I think you're the only guy who's ever asked me that. You want to know about my interests, and you don't care what I look like?!

ERIC

Yes. And I'll ask you again if you don't answer pretty soon

VOICE

OK. I don't know where to start. I don't really do much of anything, really. I just sort of, exist, y'know?

ERIC

I think so...

VOICE

I guess the only thing I really do for enjoyment is retreat. I like to hole up in my room and just be alone with myself. I'm at my most creative when there no disturbances.

ERIC

You write?

VOICE

Try to, but I never quite get to the point. There's just too much going on.

ERIC

That's one of the laws that govern your young world. You'll get over it, trust me.

VOICE

And what makes you so sure? You're not some greasy old man, are you?

ERIC

Would it matter?

VOICE

Would it matter to you if I turned out to be a greasy old
LADY?

ERIC

Hmm..gotta point there. OK, I'm NOT a greasy old man,
if that helps you out.

VOICE

It does. Where'd you go to school?

ERIC

Too much information. You might already know me.
Which means, I guess, that I might already know you too.
What if we hate each other in real life?

VOICE

We've got nothing to lose. Besides, I don't hate anybody.
Except for a few real assholes...

ERIC

And people who treat you like shit before they know you...

VOICE

And old people who drive 35 on the freeway! Listen, I've got to get going in a minute, my mom's getting pissed, but I'd like to continue later?

ERIC

Really? Sounds like a plan. When's a good time to call?

VOICE

Um...I'm going away for the weekend. I know, it sounds like bullshit, but for real!

ERIC

I believe you...seriously, with the way my life runs, it makes perfect sense. I'll call you Sunday night?

VOICE

Sounds cool. Are you going to tell me your name now?

ERIC

Nah, you'll know it's me...

VOICE

Yeah. I think we may be onto something here....How'd you get my number, anyway?

ERIC

It came to me in a dream. Talk to ya later, k?

VOICE

OK. Bye

Eric hangs up the phone and reflects for a moment before falling back asleep.

Of course, the fiction eventually comes into play, as that story ends with a multiple slaying on stage at the prom to the delight of the cheering crowd before our heroes burn down the school and make out on the lawn, causing a cop to attempt to arrest them, which made them have to kill him, effectively setting up the sequel, but I digress... I never did any of that stuff. I only wanted to. Very, very, badly. If I only could I'd set the world on fire, indeed. Back then, anyway. OK, maybe still -- a little... Goddamned brain.

" Some of my friends sit around every evening
And they worry about the times ahead
But everybody else is overwhelmed by indifference
And the promise of an early bed
You either shut up or get cut up, they don't wanna hear about it,
It's only inches on the reel-to-reel
And the radio is in the hands of such a lot of fools
Tryin' to anaesthetize the way that you feel "

Chapter 1010: March 1997

Open Letter to all Musicians:

All right, for once in your lives I want you all to shut up and listen.

Take a look at the current state of music. There are no classifications anymore. Rock is Pop, Alternative is Pop, Punk is Pop, Industrial is Pop, Country is Pop, Metal is Pop; shall I go on? It's time to realize that the main record buying public (who are too young to even know what the fuck a 'record' is) doesn't care about you, your insightfulness, you message, or your motivation. The only thing that sells records now is IMAGE. Think about it for just a minute. These are people who only stopped shopping for records at Kmart because the original alternative kids went to indies. Those same kids who started it all have no grown up and get disgusted every time they go to those old stores they used to love so much. The same store that used to be the only place to buy Big Black imports is the same store that sells 500 copies of the Goo Goo Dolls and Hootie and the Blowfish each and every day. How many shit bands get across because of their cool imagery. Maybe they act "gothic", maybe they pretend to be suicidal, maybe they pretend to be homosexuals just because their public relations people said that they should, regardless of their actual preference. Those in charge of the major labels are happy to create a world of poseurs.

Not content to let an act be themselves, the money machine creates a personality for you.

If, by accident, you manage to get signed while still maintaining your original ideals (read: integrity) you can guarantee that your record will not be promoted adequately, because the A&R guys and their team don't care much about *your* idea. If THEY had come up with the same idea, it would be the greatest record selling gimmick since Kurt blew his fucking brains out. The message sent: Don't worry about being creative, let us do it for you.

What's a musician to do? Considering you have no control over your image, you'll have to let your songs do the talking, right? Think again, as I said, the consumers don't know or care about your true personality - they want to see Barbie and Ken on stage shaking their asses. Your songs mean nothing to anyone but yourself. Disbelief? Name one song in the last 2 years that has changed your way of thinking; that has caused an emotional response based solely on the content of the music (this does not include the love song that reminds you of your old boy/girlfriend or any of that ridiculousness.) Can you do it? Getting the point yet? This is the way things are, and the way they will stay until you all realize that you're not in it for the money. If you are, great!

Go through what I described above, sell yourself to the corporate whores, go on the world tour, do what you will with your groupies, and when you're all done, washed up, no longer the next big thing but instead old news, come back and tell me how you feel about yourself. Mr. Big Man Rock Star who went from playing crappy bar gigs to headlining arenas, from living in a studio apartment alone to fucking every groupie slut from coast to coast, from being broke as hell to being rich and selfish and back again. How does it feel once the great have fallen? If, however, you do have an appreciation for the art of music, accept that you write of yourself, by yourself, and FOR YOURSELF, and you'll be much happier when it's over. Think about it. What's more important to you, your memory, or someone else's? Your *insert cheesy lyrical cliché here,* or someone else's? Understand? Make the record that YOU want to listen to. Make it sound like YOU want it to. Write about things that YOU want to talk about.

Play the chords and make the sounds that make YOU happy. Produce it yourself. If you think the vocal line should go one way, don't let any so called producer change your mind. If you hear the guitar part sounding like this and the producer says it's not commercial or it's all wrong or any other excuse, tell him/her to go fuck themselves and continue on with your work. Does this make any sense? Your music is a piece of you. Why should this joker tell you how it should sound? Does he give a fuck about the girl who broke your heart?

Does he care that you "wanna rock"? No, all they want to do is have some fun at your expense, (read: record advance) and then charge you up the ass for it all later. The music industry, much like the government, is filled with $50.00 pizzas and $200.00 cartons of cigarettes. Think long and hard about giving up the rights to your records in hope of making lots o' money. Would you sell your baby for a million dollars? How about ten million? What's the difference between a human child and a musical composition? To a true musician, there is none. Explore the analogy. Treat your music as if you had physically given birth to it. Respect it. Keep it safe from those who would cause it harm. Help it survive in the real world.

Don't trade it for a bag of weed and a two dollar whore because once you come down from the high and your nut has been blown, what do you have left? The best you could hope for would be absolute zero, and it's all downhill from there.

The moral of the story is much more simplistic than it seems. Do everything you can to protect yourself and your children. Trust no one. Thieves and liars lurk behind every golden deal. The clouds are not lined with silver, it's really the cheap spray-on shit they coat "Platinum" record awards with. Stay true to yourself, you know the difference between right and wrong. Follow the path that is right for you.

Trial and error gets you right back where you started, so don't be afraid to try. Disappointment only makes you and your babies stronger.

Easy 'success' will turn you against your friends, your family, and yourself. The same kid you used to sit and jam with in you basement will wind up being your roadie, and you will undoubtedly treat him like shit and degrade him in front of your new 'friends' in the industry. Look to the past for inspiration. The image was there, but a band was not afraid to make a record that didn't sound like their last hit single. Personality goes a long way. Feed and nourish your children, make them strong enough to stand on their own, make them more important than you. Then and only then will you reach your goal.

Are you asking yourself who the hell am I to be saying all this? Good, maybe you understand after all. For the record, no, I haven't made any "hits", haven't gotten rich from my music. I never will, because I write for me and only me.

If you like it, fine, if not, I don't care, because it simply wasn't meant for you. It's a soul thing, you wouldn't understand. Think about it, what are your songs about? What the mailman did today? How the neighbor's life sucks? No, they are your personal experiences, why should anyone else understand and feel the way you do?

Take all this rambling and burn it if you want. I'm not really trying to give advice. I'm just telling you what I've seen happen — what I see happening. If you simply ignore it, that puts you in the same place as the 98% of the population that considers themselves "Alternative."

Apathy runs the show...be last in line to get your ticket like a good little slacker.

Let's tell the story of Atlantic City. I guess that's what you get for going to Not Quite Vegas – what happens *there* eventually comes out. First of all, let's place this event on the timeline. It was 1998. I'd just finished my year off with Amy. I'd spent a lot of time and taken a lot of care to get myself in shape. I still had work to do, but overall, I was there. I'd even gone back to work, thanks to Eric convincing me to give the Primeau's another shot. They'd eventually turn out to screw me over as I always figured they would, but later for that.

I'd even managed to get a girlfriend – again, thanks to Eric. Well, Eric's girlfriend, anyway. She had a friend etc, etc. I saw her picture, thought to myself, "not TOO bad, I can deal with that" and we were off. A few months into our relationship and I was hooked. We only saw each other on the weekends, and that was just about the perfect amount of together time.

My boss wanted me to go to AC with him to help run the show on a big real estate conference. We did this same show every year, and this year it was my turn to go. I was the low man on the pole, but Ed saw it as a great opportunity. He was a schmoozer. I was not. This was going to suck. A week alone with these idiots in a hotel filled with even more pretentious real estate people. Yay! To make matters worse, this was the very weekend that my girlfriend would be attempting to move into my house with me.

The day I got back from the convention. Into my basement, actually. Just perfect for me - alone. Not so perfect for two people. Not at all.

Anyway, I was doing my usual hide and sulk routine, when Ed called me to come down. We were going to go out and find something to eat after working all day and just try to relax a bit while we had a chance.

We wound up at the Hard Rock Café, which is always pleasant for me. There's something about all the memorabilia. A link to the past. A million demons trapped and freed through the artifacts stored in that room. Plus, Gene Simmons' Dragon Boots! We were finishing up our drinks when the people who ran the real estate company walked in. Kissing ass, my boss invited them to our table. Damn, Ed...

After a few more drinks and a lot of talking and goofing around, I noticed I had a girl giggling on my arm. This was new! So - I broke away from the group and the two of us hit the boardwalk. We did the usual stuff two slightly wasted people would do when alone together on the boardwalk. It didn't take too long to figure out what was going on here, even for a brain as screwed as mine.

Problem was, my girlfriend was moving into my fucking house two days later. A commitment my brain had already made for life. Goddamned brain, here we go again.

I made it all the way to her door. The elevator ride up was the most trying experience of my life. I knew I couldn't do what I wanted. How unfortunate! I'd found a girl who was into me, and was super cool, and who I thought was incredibly hot! Now, I was about to say goodnight, without even taking the kiss that was right there in front of me. Because I knew I wouldn't want to stop there. I was invited in, but I said goodnight and left her standing in her doorway wondering what the fuck my problem was.

Maybe *that* had been the problem right along. Was I chasing everyone away by not reacting properly? After all, if you see someone pick up a hammer, and start whacking themselves with it..... are you going to feel sorry for them, or are you going to step away slowly, and hope you don't get their attention?

Wonder is all I have. I wasn't married. Ed was telling me what a dumbass I was for even thinking about passing up a sure thing. I wasn't married – but I just got my first girlfriend ever, and I've only known her two months, and she's moving into my room. I still had romantic ideals. Naïve idiot, eh?

Even better? My wife has told me on numerous occasions that she wishes I HAD gone for it that night. To clear it up. To get it out of the way. She's even gone so far as to give me permission to do whatever it takes in the future.

Because it still bothers me 30-40 times a minute... Even if it caused us to break up, maybe that would've been the right thing.

Who knows what might've happened? Not me. Oh well. I'm learning... More input!

That girl called me a couple times over a couple weeks after we got back to town. She was asking about easy computer stuff. Making random conversation trying to get me to say *something*. I'm pretty sure I was supposed to ask her out at some point. From this vantage point, it's rather obvious what she really wanted. I didn't realize that until many, many YEARS later. Years! I'm good like that! I'm aware of the problem and I'm *still* oblivious to things like that. I simply can NOT pick up on flirting. Not until long after it's over. I'm flawed. Thread kill.

Chapter 1101: The Crux of the Biscuit

What I've managed to leave out so far should be glaring at this point. I've talked a lot about all the bad things that happened to me in (or around) relationships. I've said a lot of things that detail my various unhappinesses. What I need to do is tell you the story of how I met a girl and wound up married.

It's not all bad, you know. We fight and carry on, and I know there's probably something better for each of us, but we've been together for so long, and done so much for each other, that it would just seem weird to be apart. We'd manage, but it would seem weird. Better? Maybe. Weird? Certainly.

When I was finishing up the big personal improvement kick of 1997, my friend Eric had just started seeing Dorinda - the woman who would eventually become his wife. She was having a party at her house and invited me over. Eric and I had been through a lot, and now that he was happy, he wanted me to be happy too. There were going to be a few girls there that Dorinda said would be interested in a guy like me.

Sounds good. I'm there! So, I put myself together and off I went. The party didn't wind up going so well that night. Almost no one showed up for one reason or another.

No girls at all. One semi-random guy I'd never met (who went on at great length to warn me away from the girl Dorinda was about to introduce me to... Nerd, did you fuck my wife? Grrr..) and one of Eric's other friends.

Total guy fest. We hung out. Dorinda started showing me pictures. I've told this story somewhere else, but I looked at the pictures, thought (and basically said,) "Not too bad. Certainly better than nothing! Hook me up!" and she emailed her friend to tell her to contact me, because I sure as hell wasn't going to make the first move. Yes, I'm good like that. For sure.

I forgot about it right away, but a few days later, I got an interesting email. It was Jaimee. She'd gotten Dorinda's email, maybe seen my picture, I'm not sure. Either way, she was interested enough to start talking. We sent pages and pages of email back and forth. Long distance calls were still extremely expensive then. The internet was a cheaper, longer lasting form of contact. I thought it was great! I could finally get to know someone – not only without them being able to see me, but with no voices involved to confuse or betray me.

I still think that she fell in love with the guy who's typing this. The voice inside that handles all the text based stuff. He's a lot more smooth and suave than the real life individual that surrounds him. I'm sure I revealed my secrets gradually. So gradually that the problems snuck up and took her by surprise.

I've always been this way, but I'm so good at hiding it, that we were married several years before she ever knew the deal.

We talked and talked while sitting 99 miles away from each other. Slowly getting to know each other. Slowly falling in love. Quickly jumping to sex! Woohoo! Second actual date, I was in there, buddy! It's funny now, but man was I stressed out! Without getting too far into pornoland, let's say that it was no one's finest performance. It took us FOREVER.

I don't know who these movie people are, who are always embarrassed by lasting 5 seconds during sex, but after 2 *long* days of trying, I was getting nowhere. The action was taking place, it just didn't feel like anything. What the hell is going on here? Is THIS it? Seriously? I've spent 13 years trying to do this and this is it?

That explains the questions I have now. I know that's NOT a typical reaction. I want to know *why*. It could be my brain. It could be the girl. I may never know.

Of course, I've (in fact, we've) gotten better at it since. She's got no complaints. I *know* what I'm doing. We've had plenty of practice. It's still not "right" though. It's not a question of "good", but it's not *right*. I can't explain it any better because I don't fully understand it myself. I *need* another example to form my hypothesis.

Not understanding something about myself is the quickest way to send me over the edge as I start to feel confused because how can there be something about me that I don't understand and how can I fix it and what's wrong with me anyway I just…

I just did it again. Damn. Calm it down…

What you can gather from all of this (and the rest left untold) is that we don't hate each other. We don't want each other dead. We try to do nice things for each other whenever possible. We just have no time for one another. She needs people around all the time, I need people to stay away. She feels lost and afraid when she's alone. I feel lost and afraid when I'm not. Except when I'm with the *right* person, I notice I can feel safe, secure, and happy - and the problems go away for a bit.

The problems *don't go away* when I'm with her. I don't know why. She doesn't soothe me, for some reason. I can't give you anything specific. We just don't lock together that way. It seems like she resents my problems more than anything. I resent my problems too! Then we argue it out in my head, give each other a group hug, and go back on the defensive. You know what happens when you bitch at me for being anti-social? I get *more* anti-social. Then the arguing starts. It's really hard to win an argument with me. You're fighting against a team of trained professionals, for one. I can attack virtually any statement and turn it around on whoever spoke it.

You don't want to get in a pissing match with me. Verbal attack is my specialty. I KNOW how to make you cry. If you give me two or three sentences, you will. Words are my weapons! Unfortunately, she's especially vulnerable to verbal attack. Her childhood hadn't been as pleasant as mine. I went home to escape school. She went to school to escape home. Lots of yelling and screaming went on in there, from what I've heard through the years. Not a happy place to be, in general.

In turn, she tends to withdraw and get quiet and never come out and tell anyone what's actually wrong. I literally have to start arguments on ridiculous subjects sometimes, and push and push until I finally make her cry (it's a skill...) Otherwise, she keeps everything inside and gets no emotional release at all. That's FAR more 'unhealthy' for you than what I've got going. If nothing else, I know how to vent. If you piss me off, you're going to know about it, extensively, until I feel better. I keep too much other stuff bottled up to hold on to things like *that*. There's simply no room for it.

How do you think that makes ME feel? Having the *goal* of making someone break down – making them so sad that they simply can not hold it in anymore – it's not a fun feeling (usually...)

We had our biggest split shortly after we were married. I was taking medication to fix the brain problem. It seemed to be working well enough. I was doing better on day to day stuff.

Going out, getting things done, that kind of thing. One of the many unfortunate side effects of those meds is an uncontrolled desire to not give a shit about anything. The *entire purpose* of that stuff is to make you relax and not worry so much about every little thing and to keep you calm in the face of whatever it is that usually disturbs you.

It made *me* not care what the balance was on my credit card. I'd always paid off whatever I'd purchased the minute the bill came. Now it was a different story. Without the voices telling me everything was wrong, I'd gone to the other side. *Nothing* was wrong! I spent and spent until I reacquired all the childhood possessions that had escaped me – either through breakage, loss, or mom throwing my shit in the trash when I wasn't looking.

All in all, I spent about $20,000 in those few months. Yep. Seriously! Then the credit card companies did what they do best, and my $20k worth of goods suddenly turned into $40k worth of debt. Fuck! And we'd only been in our house a few months – which cost a hell of a lot more than we'd figured. Groceries are expensive. Supplies are expensive. Insurance is expensive as hell. We had $10,000 to put down on the house when we bought it, and at the end of the day, after fees and whatever, we put $500.00 towards the price of the house. No problem, the mortgage won't go up THAT much. It didn't.

What we didn't know was that the insurance and tax that would be added in there every month were almost as much as the principle.   To break it down to simple dollars and cents, after 5 years of paying $1100 every month towards our 30 year mortgage, our principle loan amount decreased from $105,900 to $105,000.   Fuck me.   Do that math. $66,000 dollars we sent those people, in five years, for them to take $900.00 off our tab.   Never again. Fool me once.   We tried to sell the house before the market got really bad.   Too late. It's still sitting there.   Empty and devastated.   I think the bank has claimed it back at this point. Not sure. Doesn't matter.   I wish it had never happened in the first place. Money had screwed us slow, hard, and deep.

Once I learned we were going to have a baby, I knew we had to get out of there as soon as possible.   I finally convinced my grandmother to ask her tenant to leave. That lady had been there over 20 years, and was still paying 20 year old rent.   She was starting to make more demands of my grandmother as well.   This is broken, that is leaking, etc.   At some point, she must've had enough, because she agreed with me.   After the house was empty, we cleaned it all up, new paint, new floor, all the good stuff.   We used the baby room as storage, but over the next few months it would slowly become a nursery.

Things moved so fast, we never really had a chance to sit down and talk any further, so we're stuck in some kind of a holding pattern. Until when? Until the kid turns 18? I think not. There must be a better solution. Right?

Chapter 1110: A New Hope

I was at my lowest point ever. Two people who meant the world to me BOTH died within 3 weeks of one another. Bam. No time to think about it. No time to deal with it. No time for my fucked up brain to slowly process and cope. It was like taking two shots to the head as far as my psyche was concerned. So here I sit, no one left in the world but me and my kid (and my now equally screwed up mother, but that's someone else's book.) I have no one left in the world to talk to, I exist to take care of the baby. He's only 7 months old and doesn't know the meaning of "hold on!" I attempt to sleep in 15 minute increments whenever possible. My dreams, which were my escape – my safe haven – have been taken from me, as I never get far enough asleep to enter a dream state. I'm slowly dying. I'm being forced out of my mind. I tell my wife constantly "You people are killing me!" but she doesn't seem to understand. Or maybe she'd just prefer me to be gone. Whatever.

I withdraw into myself, but work must continue. I can't bring myself to get dressed anymore. I go everywhere in sweatpants and slippers. I notice I'm wearing the same outfit as Bob Dennis, and I know I can't go on like this. I decide it's time to quit my job altogether and just hole up in the basement and recuperate. I have one last class starting tonight, and then it's all over. I'm going to give up all hope, and just let them take over.

The voices couldn't help me with this, because they were all tied up trying to cope right along with me. We were *all* totally fucked.

If I simply stop fighting it, eventually I'll go completely insane, and then I won't have to worry about anything ever again. They'll either lock me away and medicate me until I'm comatose for the rest of my life, or my body will give up along with my brain and I'll just fall over dead for no reason. Whatever. I just can't go on like this anymore.

What do you know? The studio owner booked a session over our class – again. It happened all the time, it was a matter of financial need, to be honest -- but this was not the right moment. So I'm running around frantically trying to make some order out of this mess. I've got a room full of students asking me what's up, a bunch of someone else's clients asking me what's up, and now – some band walks in and tells me they're scheduled for my class. What the hell? No one schedules my bands except me! It takes me a minute to recognize him, but I know this kid! No wonder Marty booked them.

I'd met Adam a year or two ago through an old friend of mine. I knew he was interested in music and recording, but didn't know he had gotten a band together. To be honest, I hadn't heard much about him in quite awhile and he'd pretty much fallen off my radar. It happens.

But yeah – I'm interested in hearing what this guy has got for me. He always seemed cool enough, he was a friend of Tom's, he went to a Cure gig with us – he can't be all bad. He was apparently motivated enough to call us up and set up a session, so why not? I'm in the office trying to deal with a frantic stack of paperwork when he brings the rest of the band in to meet me.

Adam was working his guitar player charisma thing as hard as he could, so I could tell he'd be right at home in the studio. The rhythm section guys didn't make much of an impression that first day, to be honest, but I'll never forget the moment I first heard the words, "Hi! I'm Crystal!"

What's this? A girl in the band? Interesting. And she clearly knows no fear if she's willing to approach *me* like *that*. No reservations. No holding back. Pure energy. I'd always had a good time recording female voices because there's so many ways to approach it. Now I *really* wanted to hear some of their stuff! Unfortunately, it would have to wait. We had no studio. It was the 27th of June. The following week we were off due to the 4th of July holiday. It would be two weeks before we got back in the studio.

7/11/2006 - The first week of a new class. My first session with a new band. I was in a large room with 15 strangers and one former acquaintance. I didn't even have an assistant to rely on if things got rough. No familiar faces, nowhere to run and hide. Ouch.

I did the usual thing.   Got the band set up.   Got the students setting up mics.   Reset all the mics myself because these students were fresh from another instructor's class, and he couldn't mic to save his life. Especially not while sitting on the couch, which was all he ever did.   Everything's ready and Adam asks me for a couple of vocal mics, because they want to sing live along with the music.

In the studio world, we usually try to avoid that sort of thing, especially when teaching first week students, but he said they needed to hear the words to know where they were at in the song, so I set them up.   The only two mics left in the building, they weren't the highest quality devices.   In fact, they were $10 pieces of shit.   It wouldn't matter...

After much screwing around and the usual student mishaps, we were ready to record.   I hit the button, give them the signal and...

Guitar intro.   Nice!   Looks like this dude can play!   The band kicks in and the sound is upbeat and happy.   When four young people walk into the studio in 2006, you're expecting some emo crap to come out.   I'm kinda digging this.   Joey the Drummer Guy is grooving hard, Jadon the Bass Player is happily bopping along.   The class couldn't care less, but fuck them.   Ignorant little pricks.

I'm doing my little producer guy dance in the control room and – when the first vocal line hit, my brain was transported to another place. A place where I could see a possible future.

What I was hearing was absolutely mesmerizing. Raw, powerful, emotional. Sure, there was room for improvement, there always is, but this was something special! It could've been something hallucinogenic I'd absorbed off the surface of the console, which had lived through many a George Clinton / P-Funk session, but I'd swear to you, I saw new colors and lights when she sang. Something in that sound had penetrated layer after layer of defenses and unlocked some previously sealed off portion of my soul. Goddamned brain...what else are you hiding away from me?

As we got to the solo section, I came back to reality and saw Adam shredding out in that big wooden room, playing something between an 80's metal solo and something he picked up from an old ska tune. Undeniably his own sound, which seemed to be made up of all my favorite bits of guitarists past. The sounds of his guitar – the tones of her voice – the whole mixture of sonic goodness being formed in that room was speaking directly to the core of my brain – my *soul* -- jacked in directly to the essence of ME. What the hell?

I'd worked on a *lot* of records, made a lot of music. This, however, was my new reason for existing.

They were everything I needed and I could be everything they'd need. This was the one. Together, there would be nothing that could stop us.

I went home that first night completely revitalized. No longer would I have to simply sit there, impatiently waiting out the days until I would finally cease to exist. I had something to live for. Something to accomplish. People who needed me. I loaded up the tracks into the computer and began to do the thing I do.

The hundred days we spent making that record could tell a story of their own. In fact, they did! Go buy the CD, you'll figure it out. It's all laid out right there. Lots of thinking, lots of drinking, lots of exploring, and lots of ignoring. Long story short, that much time together in small dark areas working on these musical extensions of ourselves had formed a bond. By the time the CD was released, we knew (or I knew, anyway) that this would be something we could do – would want to be doing - for the rest of our lives – together. We had become family. Five brilliant minded lost souls against the world.

We're coming for you next...

Touring is bound to be rough on me. I pulled it off when I was 18, but how about now? I can tell just from attending gigs that it's not going to be simple. The overload present at a typical bar gig is indescribable. See, people tend to accuse me of being an asshole, or cold, or distant, or whatever when I don't engage in conversation at these things. Here's my thought pattern in that situation – no punctuation added because I would have none helping me.

"OK there's a bunch of people over there playing pool there's two guys at a video game there's about 25 people across the room in the other section oh man someone's talking to me I can't hear them well because I have to keep these earplugs in there's a band playing right there dumbasses if everyone wore them we could all hear or maybe they could just turn it down but whatever ok answer the question you were just asked cool now see what this other person has to say oh great someone else to meet and remember and whatever hey where are the members of the band I see samantha over there so adam must be nearby joey is setting up his drums oh here comes patrick he must need another drink and yay heres another person I don't know trying to talk to me for some reason I wish these people would go away I really don't need this right now there's crystal she must've been out front trying to sell some merch she does way too much for us and where the hell is jadon I'm going to walk away slowly now and join them before anyone tries to stop me again ok bye here I go...."

The above conversation takes place in my mind over the course of approximately 30 seconds. Refreshed every 30 seconds. EVERY 30 FUCKING SECONDS!

You probably can't come close to *reading* it all out loud in 30 seconds. It's like having a bunch of two year olds in my head asking "What's that? Why? Why? Why? No! What's that? No! What's that? Why? NO!! Ok..." Always. So much fun...and I get to enjoy it each and every time I'm in the presence of new people. Everything ceases to bother me once my band starts playing for me. When we're together, I'm invincible! *We're* invincible. It's *before and after* that hurt. It won't stop me from doing it though. We can do anything we want if we put our minds to it. – and stick together, because we're all we have, once again. It always comes down to me and mine against the world for all the marbles. What we're going to do with those marbles once we get them, no one knows...

OK, now this is interesting... For some reason, I decided it was time to share some of this stuff with someone. There were only a few potential choices. I chose the three people I considered least likely to hurt me, and edited each of them their own version. Everyone didn't need to know the same stuff. One person got everything, another about 60%, and the third got around 25%. From the time I delivered their virtual packages until I started hearing back, I went from relatively calm to "oh my god what the fuck have I done?!" in about three and a half days.

There's a lot of ME in this book! I was concerned that they might read some of that stuff and freak out and pull away. You never know. I selected these people to confide in because I figured they'd be least likely to do that, but you never know – and the waiting is always the hardest part. Thank you, Tom Petty, for teaching us that very wise lesson.

First to report back said it made them fall apart a bit, but mostly wanted to know how they could help. Give me space when I need it, know why I leave when I do, and try and understand what's going on a little better. Same advice I always give, basically.

The second person thought it was a good story, but didn't seem to have an opinion much beyond that. She wanted to read more, presumably to know how the story ends. Think about who this might be for a minute. You won't be surprised...

The third person was taking a minute to get back to me, but that was a lot of text, and it takes a lot of time to soak in and process. Nevertheless, in the back of my head, there was a small but vocal group telling me that I shouldn't have crossed that line.

Too much information. When the response finally came, it took me a minute to open it up.

I had to prepare myself a bit. Like the lady or the tiger routine – what would be behind the door when I opened it? Understanding? Or condemnation?

What I discovered was unexpected, but made a lot of sense. Not only did they understand, but I got a long wall of text right back that let me inside *their* head! That's all the info you're going to get here, because, once again, that's someone else's book, should they care to write it. And they should – because it really helps. A lot.

Wow! Is this what that "openness" thing is about? What sharing your innermost secrets with another human being feels like? It was amazing how similar our mental conditions were! Not for all the same *reasons*, but that's beside the point.

I don't think I'd ever felt as good in my life as I did at that moment. Not even the first time I held my son, because he was so tiny and fragile, I was afraid I'd break him.

I didn't – but he damn near broke me over the two years that followed. I hope he appreciates me later, but I won't hold my breath.

Hours later, the feeling is still there. I wonder how long I can hold onto it before the walls crash down again? What will be the thing that sets it off? What will be the next thing to attempt to break my spirit and tell me that I'm a useless good for nothing again? Always having to fight with yourself can really be a drag.

There are things going through my head right now that would probably become easier if I'd just admit to them – to myself, at least. Admit? Or commit? I know what could soothe the beast, but not knowing what brand new demons may spawn keeps me on lockdown. It suddenly occurs to me that someday, I may look back on all this and smile. I sure hope so. Things always look better when they're in the past, don't they?

Time hasn't failed me quite yet. I'm starting to wonder if it's not as linear as we think. I have a feeling that time eventually curves back upon itself – via making you experience the same things, over and over, until you find a way to break the cycle. I may be onto something here – but how does one break a cycle? I suppose it's a bit close to that Bill Murray movie, but is it *that* far out there? That the universe would force you to remain in place, repeating your mistakes over and over until you finally figure out how to live correctly?

Seems to me like that's *exactly* how it works. Only it takes place over generations. We're not repeating *our* mistakes – we're repeating our parents' mistakes – and their parents', and so on into infinity. Until someone figures out a way to escape the trap and alter the path. By doing something wildly unexpected and totally unbelievable, thus solving the universe's tricky little puzzle in the process.

It's not the things you do that screw you over, it's the things you DON'T do. Oh. I just learned that as I typed it, people. That never really occurred to me before. It's true, isn't it? Being afraid to do things – to take chances – to give living a chance – has been the problem right along. Could it really be that simple? Time to start trying things again. I *used* to try things...when I was 5...

Each and every time I go up the stairs, I can count on having an argument of some sort. Or having something piss me off. Or an argument about something having pissed me off. Whatever.

I've managed to get in a good mood several times today alone, and when I go upstairs to get something or another, BAM! Something I'm doing isn't right, or I'm not paying enough attention to her, or I'm paying *too much* attention to her, or I'm not watching the kid enough for her, regardless of the hours I've already spent with him, and the fact that he's sick of me after a full day and wants to see his mom.

She's more interested in the fucking TV. Seriously. She's mad because she has to spend time with Tom and can't watch her fucking Harry Potter interview – which is *recorded* and will wait until time is available. Can you imagine? Maybe after spending hours on end with him, I might feel that way. In fact, I frequently do – after being with him from 9-5, I'm ready for some alone time. She's only been home 4 hours, and he spent an hour of that in his room napping, and another hour trapped in his chair at dinner time. What the fuck... She gets home at 5, he goes to bed at 11. 6 possible hours! Minus a one hour nap! 5 possible hours to spend with him out of the entire day and she wants LESS. And for this, I continue to deny myself?

I swear, right now, on my entire 5 ft. stack of first pressing Zappa, KISS, Prince, and/or Cure LPs (I consider those holy artifacts as one would a bible, I'd imagine. Music, love, thought, and energy are what I'd consider my "God". The collective well wishes of those who created for the love of creating - going forth to inspire and motivate others. That's why religion was created, right?) – anyway...

If I EVER find out that the person I adore feels the same way, even if only enough to give things a try – once – for a single moment in time -- I will do so, and accept whatever happens with a smile on my soul for the first time since forever. Honestly. I've made a deal...

Today – tomorrow -- five years on -- fifteen years – whenever. I can wait. I've proven that. No hurries, no regrets. I already foolishly gave up one chance - years earlier - and I'll never do it again.

It's rare enough that I like someone enough to talk to them to get interested in the first place. I can't waste time jerking around anymore. There's the nagging problem – you never know when your time is going to come. I've witnessed it first hand.

There was nothing *seriously* wrong with John, until he fell over dead. My grandmother was getting old and had trouble using her remote control to be sure, but she showed no signs of serious failing. Wearing out, sure, but not *failing*. She felt weird one Thursday night. I told her she should probably go to the hospital if she felt weird enough to be concerned.

They found utter devastation throughout her body and mind. Just like that, she had a week to live. Just two weeks earlier, I had told her she was nuts when she told me "I'm next, you know" after John's funeral. Yeah. That's not a particularly fond memory.

This was a person who went to a doctor or two each week, who'd had every test imaginable at some point or another. There's NO way that went undetected, yet somehow, *it did*.

So I feel a little less invincible – knowing that no matter how careful you are, or how safe you play it, at some point, when you're least ready for it, you're going to die. Fucking sucks.

I hope my last thought on earth isn't "Why didn't I tell her when I had the chance?" because that would just suck for all eternity – or whatever.   Fuck wasted opportunity! I already panicked once.

I got a message one morning that I was certain was going to end tragically and started to panic before I even finished reading it. I thought "Oh my god! What if that's it? She could've died right there! And I'd never get a chance to talk to her again – to tell her how I felt – to tell her how much she really meant to me…"

I'd considered the possibility that something could happen to *me*, but this was far worse.   I get closer to making the leap on occasion, but c'mon… read between the lines.   You know what I'm *really* afraid of screwing up, don't you? Don't you.

Will I ever tell her? I wonder, but I think not – I tell myself there's no way - I can't fuck up and help ruin someone else's life – thus, the 'treading lightly on broken glass' approach. But you just *know* there's going to be a little voice that has something to say about it…and it's interesting to reread the last few bits and realize I shifted from worrying about *why* to do it to worrying about *whether* to do it.

We'd have to both be so out of it that we could pretend it never happened. Or maybe just so *into* it, that nothing else matters. How delicious... Maybe it's not so cut and dried after all.

I'm sure when it's all said and done, I'll think things over a million times and consider all the possibilities before making a decision – and discovering there are possibilities I've ignored. What I *won't* be doing is getting upset about it – stressing out over it - either way. I'm good at keeping secrets...and time is bound to be on my side, sooner or later, as long as I refuse to give up. I've got to keep trying.

"You gotta fight for your right to party!"

I've known that for 20 years! I should probably give it a try - and quit worrying about everything so much.

I'm trying to sort things out with my mother. There shouldn't *be* anything to sort out, but whatever. I didn't do it. I'm still me. We're having the same conversation today we had six months ago! See, and then I tell people they're not listening to me and they disagree! Don't argue when you can't win.

Here's what I said then: .

=======================

I don't want you to do anything other than understand that I don't like to hang out much with anyone - and it has nothing to do with you or anyone you know personally. You seem to be taking this the wrong way... I don't know how else to explain. The only reason I don't come over more is because that's what I do.

I keep saying the same things.. I haven't changed. Still doing the same stuff. You've changed everything, and the new you just doesn't like the old me as much as the old you did, I guess. I'm a downer. Party-pooper. Sorry - I get overwhelmed at gatherings -- crowds cause me panic. I had to bolt out of there and find the band the other night because I was being surrounded by people wanting to talk to me about shit I didn't want to talk about and the music is banging and they expect me to talk and I have to take my earplugs out and that REALLY pisses me off and if I keep typing I can start having a panic attack all over so I guess I should stop, but -- what do you want me to do differently ? ? ? ? ? ? ? ? ? ?

Here's what I said today:

=====================

Now that you read all that other stuff, maybe the above makes more sense. It should. I was basically trying to tell you then. I told you in 1997, 1991, and 1986 as well, though in different ways. "Why don't you want to go to school? Why do we always have to fight to get you to do _____? Why do I have to tell you the same thing 50 times? Why aren't you listening when I'm talking to you?" Dealing with this is nothing new for me, but it seems you're reluctant to accept it. It's not your fault. It has little to nothing to do with you, other than the hereditary possibilities. Nonny likely had the same thing. She had people in her head telling her she was no good, not to try anything, not to leave the house and eventually they made her a hermit and ate her brain. Nana was a nutball in so many ways, we don't even need to get into it. She lived with that thing for how many years knowing the things she knew he did? And who knows what they did that we don't ever even want to discover?

Check out this link:
http://en.wikipedia.org/wiki/Causes_of_schizophrenia

It says all the detailed stuff you could possibly want to know, but you're essentially off the hook unless you either got really sick while you were pregnant - flu, respiratory infection, etc, or were actively using some heavy shit while I was inside you. If it was either of those things, then, you win! But otherwise, it just happens. A bad electron or two in the mix somewhere.

Various experiences may have caused additional fractures, but it's mostly chemical. You gave me that movie to watch -- A Beautiful Mind -- that's the Hollywood BS version of what I have. That guy was schizophrenic -- and a brilliant mathematician who saw things in strings of numbers that normal people couldn't.

Ever watch me read upside down? Or solve Wheel of Fortune before any of the letters are revealed? Or get in trouble in school for not showing my goddamned work in math class because I could SEE the answer straight up?
I wasn't slow or developmentally challenged when the psychologist got at me when I was six, and I wasn't exactly bored. I was just off on another level entirely.

I was too distracted by the things going on in my head to pay attention to the bullshit they were trying to feed me. First grade was all about playing Candy Land and coloring, with an hour or two of math and reading at a level I'd surpassed by age 3. The most mentally challenging part of my day was the Batman adventure we acted out on the playground at lunchtime. So they'd ask a question, and a few beats later, *if I felt like it*, I'd respond. Correctly - but not at the pace they wanted.

Too fucking bad for them (which is basically what you told them, so good going!) So it was one part boredom, one part an undetected early need for glasses (did I mention schizophrenia slowly destroys the part of your brain that handles vision?) and 98 parts voices in my head telling me I could ignore the adults because they were obviously slow and developmentally challenged! Ironic...no?

In other words, I'm not like this because I'm the sad little loner boy in the corner, I'm the sad little loner boy in the corner because I'm like this. Big difference in the 'which came first' department.

You don't remember me sitting in closets with the lights off having conversations with no one? As far back as the house on Houston-Whittier?

I do.... and on Manning in the weird closet with the bare light bulb. I had an additional spare room to play in, having conversations the whole time, *alone* in the big upstairs on Doremus. I *wasn't* playing with toys. The front hall closet behind the door on Avon, usually with a video game but not always -- then it switched to the basement or under a table with a sheet over it until we moved out west, when under the sleeping bag, or the walk-in closet became the safe place to hide.

No big deal, it's always been there, I didn't know it was a "problem" until 10 years ago, and I'm not interested in 'fixing' it, so don't feel bad for me.

Not for that, anyway.   I certainly don't.

I'm glad you're happy (though in one way, you now become one of those "happy couple" people I can't be around for long.) I just told you ALL that stuff in those pages. You KNOW how I feel about things, and you know essentially why I feel that way. Until I can change that, how do you think it makes me feel that you've gone through at least 2 new people recently and I'm STILL stuck with the same one I shouldn't be with in the first place?

I'm at a point where I just don't need anything else making me feel bad. Coming to those gigs is a mixed bag. On one hand, there's something about them that makes me feel better than anything else in the world, even if only for a short time, once a week. On the other, there are a bunch of people I don't know who seem to know me which always freaks me out.

There's total auditory overload. Lights flashing etc. I worry enough about strangers and what they think, then Patrick tells me "Oh yeah, those girls in there sure fuckin' HATE you!" Because of how I "mistreat my mother" Seriously? Seriously? Hopefully not, because otherwise people should shut the fuck up about things they know not about.

Now I can't come up there anymore, because it's too much. I will though - because I HAVE to. I NEED to be there. You have no idea... No one does. No one could.

Also, I never knew you had that kind of problem with Non and summers and whatever. Maybe now that you have all this new info, it'll make a bit more sense to you. It wasn't so much the being here, or being around her specifically, as it was a) everyone else was here, there were a LOT more familiar faces to me here than in CA and b) THERE WAS NO SCHOOL WHILE I WAS HERE!!!!!

When the summer vacations ended, I *had* to go to school somewhere, and it would've sucked just as bad here - probably more, because of snow and ice. Then *she* would've had to deal with all the stuff you had to deal with. If I'd have wound up with dad somehow, it would have been *his* problem. So the issue was not personal, but entirely situational.

I STILL wake up from time to time in a panic because I have to get up for school. THAT'S how fucking traumatic grades 7-12 were on me -- like they are on most everyone at this point, I'd imagine. They were no picnic for Kate or Bob, that's for sure.

I was picked on mercilessly by everyone except the 5-10 kids you ever met and / or saw at the house.

I didn't tell you all that shit, because what was the point? You'd go down there and fix it (which would be good!) but then I'd get made fun of for needing my mommy so much (which was bad - sometimes worse...)

I was fat, had the bad haircut, the crooked glasses, had the clothing issues so I wore weird shit all the time, hung around with total nerds, and didn't give a shit about the sort of things all the other kids were into - sports, clothes, shitty music, etc.

I dreaded the end of August not so much because I had to leave here (though that *was* part) but because I was SO terrified to have to go back....there.....to that goddamned place with ALL those people - watching me. I'm overwhelmed when I'm in a small crowd, or when I have to meet new people.

I had to do that 6-7 times a day - every day - that I went to school. Ever have a panic attack in front of a bunch of high school students? Doesn't do much for your rep, I'll tell you that! Again, not your fault - unless ALL the other parents are to blame too, because this same stuff affected us all - it just hit me harder due to the special brain issues. You're off the hook. Forget about it...

The only thing that really bothers me around here lately is how gross and dirty everything has gotten. I'm really concerned with the swarms of flies and gnats, the family of rats that has taken over the garage and has us afraid to get near it (one of these days, they're going to eat Lily when she goes behind the garage...) There was a fucking HAWK in the yard last week. A scavenging HAWK. That is NOT a good sign. They don't come around healthy places. I have a 2 year old here who has to play out there, and I can't go outside half the time to do anything about it myself. Allergies *suck*.

We have the grass guys, and I trimmed the bushes, but beyond that, I don't know what to do other than call John and ask, and that's not going to cut it anymore. Guess I should've paid attention when he told me to, except I was too busy listening to the guys in my head talking about more immediately distracting shit.

Know why his "same 4 lines of lyrics" routine never bothered me? Because if one of those got stuck in my head, it would shut one of the dudes up for awhile... Of course, I could live without the guy that's still stuck in there singing "My hoorrrt's on faaaar for Ellllvi-rah!" but what can you do? Poop. What can we do? To get all the garbage up and kept up. To keep the food and stuff off the floor? To get the damned basement cleaned out so I might salvage whatever bit of my stuff isn't mildewed out. To burn down the garage entirely...

I'm glad you're doing well and you love your friends and all that good stuff. Why would it bother me? I don't really like when I see all the stuff that you used to care about being totally neglected in the meantime, but much of that is none of my business.

You seem to be very all or nothing at this point. Either I hang out with everyone or I don't see you. I'm not going to hang out with *anyone*.

If there's someone at your house, I'm not going to come over. I don't invite people over -- or let people know where I live - for a reason! I don't want to see them when I'm home. Home is my only remaining sanctuary. Those who I want over, have been given an open invitation. The rest? If I wanted to see them, I'd seek them out, but I don't, so stay the hell off my porch!

Get me a rocking chair and a shotgun and I'll keep those whippersnappers off my lawn!!! But seriously -- I'm civil. I talk to people when I see them. I acknowledge them. I return their chit chat, or hugs, or whatever. That's all I can do. But I certainly don't expect *you* to sit there alone forever -- That's MY job, and I've had a *lot* of experience.

	All	the	faces
"			
All	the	voices	blur
Change	to	one	face
Change	to	one	voice
Prepare	yourself	for	bed
The	light	seems	bright
And	glares	on white	walls
All	the	sounds	of
	Charlotte	sometimes "	

Yay! Another birthday... Remember how much you used to look forward to them? All your friends, presents, cake, fun times all around. It's not that I dislike them now, or have some weird feeling of getting old. On the contrary, whatever biological age my body may be, I'm still emotionally 15, so it's all good. No, the problem is that they're just not *fun* anymore. Maybe it's the difference in presents. I remember some of the classic birthday gifts – 8/3/85 kicked ass! I got both Optimus Prime AND Megatron that day! ...and the new Prince LP as well. Today, I will receive nothing but cash presents.

Nice, but it's not the same. Not that I want someone to run out and buy me toys (though if you look around, it's not at all far-fetched.) I'm just trying to point out some of the reasons why birthdays aren't as entertaining to adults as they are to children.

This year, the voices seem to be aging a bit as well. It's odd – I'd changed, but they'd always stayed relatively the same as they always were. For some reason, now, a few of them were starting to get antsy – like they were beginning to feel old! I notice it taking longer between being asked a question and giving an answer. There was always an extra beat in there, but not there were two or three sometimes. It wasn't due to confusion! The problem here was that they were fighting for control. One or two of those bastards decides to go rogue and it's up to the others to put things back in order.

The typical process is, you ask a question, I process the question, I process all the possible answers, I select an answer, I respond.

Now, the process was more like; ask, process, come up with true answer, realize that isn't acceptable, re-process, select secondary answer, commit.   There was an additional step in there, where I was essentially forcing myself into a lie.   A lie designed to trick no one but myself, because no one else would ever hear the truth to compare it to.   I'm in a delicate place here.

If I answer certain questions truthfully, I stand to hurt only the people I love.   If I continue to answer in half-truths and thinly veiled lies, I continue to harm myself.   It comes back to who I'd rather hurt – others?   Or myself?   I'm my own arch-nemesis!   It's a good thing I'm so good at hiding my true self.   Very few people can see through the veil of deception I keep in front of me.   I have to *welcome you in*, you won't get in otherwise. *Can't you hear me knockin'? Help me baby, I ain't no stranger...*

Try to penetrate my defenses and you'll get fucked up quick.   Earn my trust and respect and welcome to the party! Freddy Krueger once said "I've been guarding my gates for a long time, bitch!"   He was a bit of a crude fellow, but he was about to rip that chick's face off, so we'll let him slide.

Regardless, I know the feeling. The guarding thing - not the face ripping. I only ripped my *own* face off – never anyone else's – though I've threatened a few times...

It's time to go back into internalize mode. I've been very open lately, and it's been good. Ended some things that needed ending – strengthened some things that needed strength – made a few startling discoveries – and now? It could be all in my mind (if nothing else, we've established *that* by now) but there just may be something worth looking into here. I need to keep everything quiet until I know what I'm doing. It's so hard to *not* tell people about things that make you feel good!

The voices will take so long to sort everything out, that I'll miss another opportunity. I wish those guys would speed up their process or something. Of course, the last time I made a wish like that, I woke up 15 years later and wondered what the hell had happened.

Figure out what *that* statement means! It would take another paragraph or two, so I'm going to skip ahead and save that for the unrated director's cut of this book, coming once the regular edition isn't selling well anymore. OK? OK. Just kidding about the director's cut...

When I was 15 and feeling amazingly low, I begged my brain to just let me go to sleep, and wake me up once I had a job, and a wife, and a kid, and a house.

I woke up at age 30 saying "How in the fuck did I get here, and how do I get back to 15, when I still had a chance at life?"

Be careful what you wish for.

I don't even fucking want to get into the stuff I've seen tonight. The day started off fine. It got even better, then a few of us got a little wasted. Then it got even better! Had one of the coolest nights, got a few nice surprises, everything was going just fine. Then as quick as anything, smiles and warm fuzzies gave way to bitching and moaning, but that's nothing new. Same story, different day – and once again for no reason. Besides, if what she was mad about was *real*, we wouldn't be arguing, we'd be divorced. Obviously. If only I had the balls... Then in the middle of that, an obnoxiously drunk person comes in and kills whatever bit of buzz is remaining. It gets better. I really shouldn't even fucking type this, but after all I've already put down, who's going to complain?

There's some band guy living at my mom's house. He's apparently the most awesome singer ever (which *can't* be true, because I already KNOW the most awesome singer ever - she just left 5 minutes ago, thank you very much) and he's wonderful and whatever. I don't care, none of my business. I guess he wants to work with me in the studio or something. I was as willing as I get about anything, but it's not going to happen now. No fucking way. Without even meeting me, this guy had violated my project involvement rule #1. And it looked like he had violated it on my grandmother's kitchen table – and maybe on top of the TV too. Or maybe those $5 bills were rolled up really tight for some other reason. Whatever.

Now that I know that shit is going on over there, there's no fucking way I can let my *child* wander around over there, no matter how well supervised.

Like I fucking need him picking up something and getting powdery shit on his little hands. Yeah, that'd just fucking thrill and excite me, wouldn't it? I'd be *so* excited, I couldn't *possibly* rip someone's face off! Guess we'll never find out, because he's done with that until that guy is gone. I hope that problem leaves with him, and isn't something that's going to be there all the time, or goddamn it, I'm going to have to move again.

This is on top of the thing I tried not to witness earlier – there was something stashed somewhere on top of the TV. I'm going to hope against hope that the item was hidden in the candy box or something, because if I even THINK for a second, that someone was stashing ANYthing inside the container that holds John's ashes, I'm calling Willow and Xander, we're resurrecting his dead ass, and I'm going to let HIM go to town. Seriously – Please don't let things be devolved to the point that some scumbag is hiding drugs in with my dead father's ashes while my mom looks on. Some things are just too fucked to be reality. Where's Keith Richards when you need him?

This doesn't even get into the amount of disturbed that anyone would get from listening to their mom talk about her sexual wants and needs. There's no washing that out of your skull, people. Oh, and with my father, no less.

The one who's still living, you sick fuck! Things aren't THAT bad! See, I told you you've got to keep laughing. Otherwise you have to admit to the fact that the entire universe is completely out of whack, and there's nothing you can do but attempt to find whatever other lost souls are out here in Outer Whackville, Population: You.

Unfortunately, I doubt if there are more than 50 people in our entire universe – but at least we're all super-cool to be around.

Will this be the one chapter I have to hold back when I eventually decide to go to print? Probably. Maybe not. No....*there is another.* I know of at least one more that'll have to remain forever unprinted – well, unless I actually make it happen, then I wouldn't need secrets anymore. I can see the road in sight, but I can't get past the thought that it's the same old trap attempting to pummel me one last time. The thought pattern is: "You think? Really? REALLY? No. Of course not. Really? But maybe? No. Shut up. Forget it. Think again. Remember? You're positive? SHUT the fuck UP!!! Forgetitforgetitforgetitforgetit!!" Figure *that* one out, smeghead! I feel like Indiana Jones trying to solve the puzzle before he gets decapitated. Sometimes, you just have to walk off the edge and have faith that there WILL be ground there when you need it. I'm learning. I'm beginning to test that theory, as any scientist would – in fact, *must.* And my brain is nothing if not scientific in nature.

I've always been a learner. I absorb. I *never* study. Never have. Never will. Never needed to. I don't have a photographic memory, but rather *empathetic*. I remember the emotions and the feeling of a scene, and from there can pick out the details. I don't *see* it, I *feel* it. Sometimes I feel I start arguments with people just so I can feed off their anger, frustration, and pain. A psychic leech who has to get your emotions up before feeding. A smegging Polymorph! Bonus points if you get that one. But it's true – I'm a master of manipulation!

You know how I learned so much about taking care of kids before having one of my own? I spent a lot of time with my cousins. From the time Bobby was born, we liked hanging around together. I was only 10, so my baby care skills were limited at best. No diapers, that's for sure! We played – learned – had fun. We were happy to see each other, and he behaved better for me. His parents were happy to have a break when I'd come over. I can certainly understand that, having a 2 year old of my own.

I only got to see him during the summertime, because I was 2500 miles away the rest of the year. Still, he didn't forget me while I was gone.   A few years later, Kate came along. I was there at the hospital hours after she was born. I'd just gotten into town. It was June 1989. The summer of the first Batman movie! The Cure had just released Disintegration three weeks prior.

I was a moody goth mod 10th grader loner. And here was this tiny little baby – the smallest thing I'd ever seen. Bobby was born in November. The first time I saw him, he was seven months old. Hardly a newborn at that point. Kate had only been breathing an hour or two. An itty bitty person that looked like a wet pink prune.

Now I had two of them to hang with. Bob was 4 ½ when Kate was born. He was fairly capable of handling most of his needs for himself. Didn't need diaper assistance anymore, could get simple food and beverage tasks taken care of.

He could load and program the VCR quite well. He was only a few months away from starting school and he was *ready*. That didn't stop his parents from putting him in a *Pre*-K program that first year. Pissed me right off, but what could I say? I was still a kid myself.

I'd *been* that kid though! I'd been told I was "slow" and needed special training of that sort. I already told you how that worked out. Slow, I am NOT. Whatever. It didn't scar him. He turned out OK.

Sometimes I wonder if he's got the same problem I have. We've been through a lot of similar stuff, and it *does* run in families. It wouldn't surprise me if my uncle and *both* his children were like this and didn't even know about it. *I didn't* – for the longest time. It doesn't seem like a problem from the inside.

I graduated in 1991 and moved back to Michigan. Kate was only 2 at that point. At that time, I had a ton of spare time – nothing at all to do on the weekends. Nothing but class - once or twice a week at the recording school. I became an easy babysitter. I wasn't going to get into anything, I knew how to take care of things, the kids loved being around me, they could trust me. Made a lot of sense. I never minded doing it, either. Rather liked it, actually. I bonded with those kids. I took them places with me. We spent time together. I tucked them in and read to them at bedtime. We played, we learned, we read. We stayed that way for the longest time.

I even had to change my first diaper back in 1992! There was *no* escaping it that day. It didn't hurt at all. No problem!

If I had to pick a singular event that set our family off on an odd course, it would be their moving from their modest house 5 minutes away to a bigger (yet colder) place across town.

It was no longer convenient to just pop over there on the way home. Maybe that was one of their reasons for moving. Lots of people used to stop over there lots of the time.

You never know *who* someone might be willing to move away to escape from. Didn't matter. The result was the same.

My grandmother didn't see them as much anymore. That was one of the things that kept her active and happy. I think she gave up a little bit more at that point. Holidays stopped feeling the way they always had. It was more like a chore. We were all getting together because we HAD to, not because we felt like it. Everyone liked each other, we just didn't know each other anymore - or something. I don't know how to explain it. Of course, everyone probably had their own shit going on, and that certainly can affect the mood of a gathering.

Things carried on like that for awhile. Everyone went about their business and has their own things to do. Bob graduated from high school, got a job, and moved out. Kate graduated and is going through some serious crap of her own. Their parents are having a rough time. It's like we're all shooting a cliffhanger episode of some shitty 80's nighttime soap. I'm busy working on rewrites as we speak. I'm *going* to write myself a happy ending! I hope the rest of them can figure out a way to do the same.

If my grandmother *were* here, she'd bitch us all out for 10 minutes over her coffee and toast - tell us how *disappointed* she is in how our recent behavior - grab her ashtray - and walk out of the room - disgusted...

You *all* know it's true, too.

"Sixteen, I fell in love
With a girl as sweet as could be,
Only took a couple of days
Till she was rid of me.
She swore that she would be all mine
And love me till the end,
But when I whispered in her ear
I lost another friend, oh!"

I talked to my dad the other night. It might've been the first time ever, actually. Really talking. As an adult, certainly. It's not because I don't like him, or get along with him, or whatever. It's just that we either don't have or don't make the time to spend to get to know each other. That'll probably change as we both get older. It helped that I had a couple of drinks, actually. Got me talking about stuff I normally don't talk about. Put us on a similar level. Maybe made him more comfortable too. His wife wasn't home, so that might've changed the atmosphere too. I'm not sure. Whatever.

We didn't really have too much time to get into things. I'm going to have to go back and continue. He has to be in bed by 9 in order to get up at ridiculous hours for work. That would still leave an hour or two on any given day that we could get together. I'm sure he's sitting somewhere bullshitting and drinking beer, we might as well sit together. Hopefully near a pinball machine, if there is such a thing in the wild anymore.

We were doing our usual sidestepping of issues. I never really know what to talk about with him because we live such different lives. I keep forgetting we're quite similar inside. Somehow the conversation got around to mom. It was implied that she's gone a bit crazy, and he responded, "Well, I could've told you THAT!" implying it was obvious.

I showed him -- with the simple response --

"Yes, you COULD have...but you DIDN'T."

He was never really *there*. I don't think it's because he didn't want to, or because she wouldn't let him. I just think they were *so* uncomfortable together that it was easier to just stay away than to argue and fight and go through all that shit in front of me. In fact, typing that out, it seems to me that our situations are all too similar. There are so many parallels. And you wonder why I'm worried about repeating the cycle. The more we hide, the longer it takes.

No matter what I do, or how I proceed, I seem to wind up in the same traps as those who came before me. Partly because they keep whatever secrets they still feel the need to protect. At this point, I think it's more a case of not being able to live up to the hype. They've all made such a big deal about this crap for so many years (nearly 30, at this point) that nothing they could possibly tell me would be worth all the years of "ask me again when you're older." I'm older. I've asked. No response. Whatever. I'll fill in the blanks myself by reliving your past fuck ups. Thanks for nothing. Though to be honest, I don't even *want* to know at this point. Things are so fucked up in the real world around me that the past is simply not worth the runtime. I *live* in my past – I'm only happy when thinking of the past – I don't need to have an "Everything You Know Is Wrong" moment. I've already had several – how many more can there be?

That's not me tempting fate – that's me reaching an end point.   There's not much left to take away, folks – and when it's all gone, beware of what remains.   If you wind up with who I *think* you might, you're not going to like him very much...

"It doesn't matter what you do or say, just forget the things that you've been told..."

For the record, Dad, here's a recap of my story so far. You tell me if it sounds familiar.

1. Birth
2. Odd, protective parents
3. Strange childhood
4. Outsider growing up
5. Had trouble dating
6. Married first girl he slept with
7. Had kid
8. Regretted being married as other women gave him attention
9. Enjoyed excessive "partying"
10. Found another woman who made him feel comfortable and happy - and cheated
11. Screwed everything up...

I'm with you through #10, but I haven't gotten to 11 yet, so I haven't stopped to worry about 12. What was 12? Divorce? Or was there a step in between?

I just heard – from MY wife, of all people, who apparently heard from my mom – that that story could easily apply to you, Dad.

Mom was your first, right? But you weren't hers? But it didn't matter, because you were in love, and she was there for you and everything was great? Then one day, you realized *you* were better than you had realized, and noticed that other people thought so too. You were really good at what you do, and everyone was telling you how great you were. You started to party a bit too hard, and things got out of hand. Meanwhile, your wife was too busy with the kid to pay much attention to you, and she hadn't even TRIED to get back in shape after the kid was born. The kid is totally awesome, and you love him to death, but things are certainly different for you now. There was a period where you didn't get any sleep. It made you a bit crazy. Made you think about things you hadn't thought about in awhile. Made you question your decisions to that point. Sure, you'd do anything for your son, but wasn't it possible that there was another woman out there who could make you happier? And what might sex be like with someone else? It sure would be interesting to find out, wouldn't it? So one day, you find an opportunity. No, you MAKE an opportunity. No one's looking – the wife is totally preoccupied – you're in the clear. Then what? I'm right at that point, sir. That's where I can't write the rest of the story. I don't know what happens next. I can predict, based on what I DO know.

You screw the girl who makes you feel happy one night, after a few drinks and whatnot. Wow... So *that's* what it's like. Pretty much the same? Better? Not as good? That part I can't answer. Regardless, you were big enough to go home and confess. *And you were let off the hook.* That time. But the temptation was too much. Whatever you learned, it was worth trying again. And again, and *whatever*. At some point, you must've taken it too far, and she got fed up and everything fell apart. Oops. Live and learn. *And pass the fucking lesson on to your kid so he doesn't have to make the same mistakes.* There's NO reason he should have to. If nothing else, THIS was a lesson you'd learned the hard way, and if you could prevent him from making the same mistakes, it would be worth it.

Except no one's ever told me any of this. *I lived it.* I could be correct – I could be entirely off base. I have someone willing to tell me who knows the story, but didn't experience it first hand.

I sent my mom the preceding four pages in an email - seconds after I finished writing it. Here's what I said then:

"How about this bit? TELL ME.... Am I even close? Because that's MY story, and I think it's way too close to his story for comfort.

For someone who's spent his entire life trying to avoid his father's mistakes, it looks like I've done everything exactly the same. Without even knowing. Yes? No? Sorta?

You KNOW what I'm going to do next. *You do.* You've *lived* it. You've been on the short end of that stick.

So, if there's ANYTHING you'd like to tell me, right now -- RIGHT NOW -- is the time. There's not going to be any turning back in another couple weeks. Anything you can think of that you might say "Hey! This REALLY fucked things up! Avoid THIS at all costs!" to help your little dude out...

I'm leaving this book for MY kid, he'll never have any question. If he wants to avoid becoming daddy, he need only read up on the subject. *I've* wandered blindly, and apparently circled around to the same old path. I'd really like to get Tommy off this path... It doesn't need to keep repeating like this.

If you stop and think, I'll bet Grandpa G had the same thing, except he never left the scary old lady. Nonny too -- so when her husband died, she withered away one day   at   a   time.

For the record, I have someone who's GOING to tell me, as soon as I request it. I figured I'd give you one last shot.

Not being a demanding bastard, just asking for assistance if you can provide it. You can also tell me I'm entirely wrong and I'll forget about the whole thing....

thanks mom –

Her response?

"Honey I don't know what you want me to tell you. You're not like your Dad. You are your own person and Tommy is lucky to have you for a father. I tell everybody what an awesome job you do with him and how lucky he is. You're in so much pain and I don't know what to do about it. You need to do what's best for you and fuck everybody else, me included."

I really wish people would quit telling me I'm in pain. I'm not. No pain. No suffering. Just blah. I'm not technically depressed, based on how I've seen actual depressed people behave. Right now, I'm even *happy* – because I have something to look forward to for the first time in a long time. It's a nice feeling. There are a million possibilities – anything could happen. I'm learning to sit back and relax and allow myself to not have to be in control of everything all the time.

It's not going to be a quick and easy process.

Damn. I had so much to say earlier, but instead of being able to sit here and pound it out, I had to stop what I was doing and waste time. Not so terrible, I suppose. We wound up having one of those "deep" conversations – the same exact conversation, in fact, that we always have. Literally. I gave the same answers in response to the same questions. I should type THAT up, I could probably hand her the script and save myself a lot of time and discomfort.

See, I don't *want* to hurt anybody. That's just not my style. It always comes down to hurting others or hurting myself. I always seem to win the coin toss. It's easier to hurt yourself than it is to hurt others. To take one for the team. For me, anyway. It's like you don't have to feel as bad about hurting yourself because you're already fucked up. The thing we fail to realize is that everyone is just as unhappy. Other than the 1% of the population that is either rich enough to afford solutions or too stupid to notice or care, people in general are discontent. It's not just us! We've had so much practice over time that we manage to hide it better. That's the big difference.

I've been hiding so much for so long that it's become second nature. I don't think about it, it just happens. I have a tendency to hold reactions until I'm alone. Mysterious, yes. A bit of a pain in the ass at times? Surely. Sometimes I think people think I'm screwing with them – that I'm just being purposely vague or blowing them off altogether. The reality is, my poker face is on so frequently, that I rarely bother to turn it off when there are guests present, so to speak. To be honest, I spend a lot of time wrapped up in little white lies.

To elaborate is to blow my cover, so no spoilers follow, but consider the secret agent with the case full of disguises. He can put on whatever face is necessary to deal with the situation being faced – at least long enough to get to the next mission.

My poor band – I can never give them a true answer to the "How was that?" question until I've had time to absorb and process the performance. That usually means watching the video. I'm always looking for the right thing to say on the spot. Don't they know they can do no wrong in my eyes? There'd have to be one hell of an on-stage train wreck before I'd ever think a show flat out *sucked*.

Remember, I've worked shows where we had riots, gear malfunctions, stage fires, costuming mishaps, props gone wild -- the works. I've been chased out of an underground (literally!) club *without* our gear by rioting militant French-Canadians and their security guard attack dogs. Never book white guys in clown makeup to warm up 1500 non-english speaking pro-black militant hardcore motherfuckers.

They were a nice crowd, for the most part, until they saw *those two* start to rap. They played that particular show without makeup out of fear of death. I think that was the only time ever in their history that they played that way – and almost no one has ever heard about it. Just those in attendance -- and they probably don't remember at all, having not been fans... They performed wearing their leather tour jackets and street clothes. The mic stands (with the cloth bits wrapped around them Steven Tyler style) were set on fire – on stage – *while they were attempting to rap into them.*

Things went downhill from there... Those shows were still *successful* on one level or another. The true gauge of that sort of thing is the audience and its reaction anyway.

There's no reason to try and impress *me*, I'm as impressed as I'll get! Now get out there and make *those* people understand what you have that none of these other people do. A perfect technical performance given by stiff performers is not as good as a sloppy performance by energetic, charismatic individuals.

In other words, I don't care how many notes you dropped during that solo, as long as you made a cool fucking face while you did so. NEVER APOLOGIZE FROM STAGE! Did you read that? *Do NOT apologize from the goddamned stage!* You are NOT sorry. Show no sign of weakness! Fuck them! They paid to see *you*...

If you fucked up, no one knows but you and your bandmates. Ignore it and move on. Unless you've just managed to injure someone in the front row, set the club on fire or destroyed the sound system, the words "I'm sorry" should never be uttered from an active stage. Be friendly and approachable especially after the set, but *don't* apologize.

No retreat, no surrender, no remorse, no regrets!

"Now the feeling is beginning to grow
And the meaning is something you only know
If you believe it take my hand and Ill take your heart
Now I'm wondering, where does true love begin?
I'm going under so I'm letting you in"

Oh Joy! – Now my wife's trying to back out on the deal we had made. It was once determined that if we *do* separate, she could drop the kid off here on the way to work and pick him up a few hours after she gets off. Daddy Day Care – what could be better? It would be *exactly* what he's used to now. He'd wake up to Dad, spend all day here with me taking care of him, having fun, and teaching him stuff, then spend his evenings with Mom before going to bed and repeating. Just like now. He doesn't like it when we're together now, so he's usually with one or the other. This is the perfect solution to that particular problem. It *was* settled.

I mentioned that today and got "I'm not paying *you* to take care of him. Why wouldn't I just use a REAL day care then?" Ever priced Day Care services? The amount I would ask for to cover whatever wouldn't be anywhere near *that* amount, and we're talking about MY SON. Who has spent more time with me than any other human on earth. Why would his own mother think he would be better off learning from strangers than from someone who loved him? Because she's an educationally prejudiced individual, that's why. Da-Da didn't go to college, so he isn't qualified to watch baby as well as some moron with a certificate or a license– despite the fact that he's watched baby every day of his little life and done just fine so far. Watch this all have to get very dirty now - for no reason, whatsoever. And eventually, I'll have to cave into whatever winds up hurting the kid less.

She'll be more worried about screwing me over than helping Tom get by. Really nice, eh? She's not mean spirited by nature, which makes it even harder to understand. I guess I bring out the worst in her at times. I know the feeling...

I've already acknowledged the fact that I'm dead inside. I had to give up all my hopes for the future — all the things I didn't get to do when I had the chance? I no longer have the chance — but the *desire* is greater than ever. *That's* a healthy combination -- healthy like a Big Mac...

My dreams are gone, so that's out. I have no hope of things changing — unless they get worse, but I'd rather not devote any energy to that line of thinking. If I'm unhappy now, and things can't get any better, why bother? Because I still have precious time. All it would take is for the band to hit once — and we'd have enough to set us all up properly for the rest of our lives.

If I eliminate money as a concern, my life immediately becomes easier. Money can't buy me love, but it can eliminate my fear of being stuck alone — or having to go out and get a "real" job. I just don't need that hassle. I'll work my ass off and give it all I've got, but I'm not working for anyone but myself, my kid, and my band.

Get in the way of *my* efforts and get knocked on your ass for yours. We're going to make it, because we have to. It's all we have. Maybe that's what brought us together.

I was talking to one of the band members one night – a person I'd always considered relatively happy – and he told me he was glad to have something to do for once, and if the band thing collapsed, he'd be blowing his head off shortly thereafter. I thought, "Wow, he's reading my mind!" It didn't take too many drunken sessions before it was clear that we all felt this way to some degree or another.

There was nothing much to bother living for, except for this. How it had come to this, no one was quite sure, but we were drawn together at exactly the right time.

That puts a bit of pressure on me to work extra hard – to not slack -- to ensure success – because we all need to survive until that point when we can relax together and strum acoustics and do whatever the hell we please.

It's ok - I'm quite used to giving myself up to help others. I wonder what would happen if I ever decided to do something strictly because I wanted to, regardless of how it may affect others. I'd finally be happy, I'll bet. Wonder what's taking me so long? What am I afraid of? Trying? Maybe... That hasn't worked out very well so far. Then again, I hadn't tried very much – or very hard... Which is why it's so important to try now.

Decisions are a bitch. We all try SO hard, but at the end of the day, it's all about the decisions that have already been made. Decisions do not equal solutions, however, so it's entirely possible to make nothing but incorrect decisions and still succeed. It's *also* possible to think everything out, determine the best possible decisions, do everything "according to the book" and fail miserably.

Most people fall somewhere in between. With an average success/fail ratio, your brain chugs right along – business as usual. When you start to fail more frequently though, it's a slippery slope. I make informed, intelligent decisions. *I do.* The problem comes from not properly reading and interpreting other people's thoughts and emotions before making my decision. I project *my* feelings onto others in those situations – or perhaps the feelings of whichever part of me is in control at that time.

Right now, I sit here completely exhausted. Not just physically – though I could use two or three days of uninterrupted sleep – but mentally, spiritually, emotionally. I'm drained. Nothing else to tap. No second (or third...or fourth...) wind is forthcoming. It's not as hopeless as it may sound. What does one do with a power source that is completely drained? You recharge it – and it goes right back into service until it gets drained again. For all the unhappiness that's gone into these pages, and all the times I've flat out stated "I'm unhappy" there's still a lot of positivity flowing here.

At the end of the day, as long as I get time to sit – alone, in a darkened room – headphones on, candle burning -- while I let the day's worries escape for just a few minutes, everything resets and I'm just fine.   Until it repeats.

I'll tell you something I've learned about myself -- all that "doing for others" stuff is for your own benefit - because no one else even notices.   Normal people are too fucking selfish to give a shit.   Every time I've decided "Fuck this, let them take care of themselves" about *anything*, I wind up having to come in and fix an even bigger mess! Then I realized that the reason I want people around me to be happy is because that makes ME happy.

Yes, the actual problem there is that I'm an empathetic being - I feel what those around me are feeling.   That used to be normal, I guess people have "evolved" through so many eons of rotten behavior or whatever.   I don't understand what I'm taking in, it causes my brain to spit out errors.   The end effect is that I feel disconnected from the rest of the world on a regular basis.   Do you feel disconnected?   Maybe we're working on that right now.   Or not.   I could be rambling at this point.   You'll have to decide for yourself.

"For how much longer can I howl into this wind?
For how much longer
Can I cry like this?

A thousand wasted hours a day
Just to feel my heart for a second
A thousand hours just thrown away
Just to feel my heart for a second"

Strap yourself in, we're going to go straight to the center of the pain here. The exposed nerve, so to speak. If you've ever been through what I'm about to describe, you'll likely be sobbing by the time you finish this chunk. If you haven't, consider yourself blessed. *Seriously.* As a two-time survivor (who's currently about to go through it one more time – it never ends...) I can tell you that this is a feeling you're best not to experience.

Have you ever been completely, totally, heart and soul in love with someone? And they loved you right back? Only "not in that way"? More like a friend, or a sibling, or whatever? Mmm-hmm. FUCK THAT! There is *nothing* else in the world that feels like that. It's not a feeling of loss, because what you want is *right there*. Not exactly taunting you but making you *ache* inside every time you're in the same room. Knowing it would be SO great if you could just get together once.

You'd be able to prove to them how much you really loved them and everything would be fine after that because at least you'd have each other and this person is so cute and so sweet and so perfect for me and how could they possibly NOT see how great we'd be together. We like all the same stuff – we spend all our time together! We go all the same places, hang out with the same people. I'd do ANYTHING for them, and they don't seem to care at all.

Sound familiar?

I remember driving home one particularly bad morning, SCREAMING along with the song on the radio at the top of my lungs. I had suffered silently all night long, I had to have some release.

Sitting side by side with the girl I was in love with, all night long, watching her pay more attention to whatever she was fiddling with then me. Didn't she know she was absolutely perfect for me? Surely I was perfect for her too?

As someone who clearly chooses a mate based on personality over looks, it didn't occur to me that one look at me back then might have been enough to turn anyone off. Who cared what I looked like? I was a great guy! I still am....and *still* no one appreciates it at all.

Women are fucking insane. Let me leave that advice behind for my son. They always seem to prefer the painful relationship with the wrong person much more than even the *thought* of a happy relationship with the amazing person that's five feet away and totally in love with them. Guys do that too, actually. How did *that* become human nature?

I've *been* that "amazing person".

Hell, I AM that person right now!

Watching someone you're in love with -- as they're telling *you* how bad it feels to be in love with someone who doesn't want *them* -- while *that* person tells you how much they don't want to love *anyone at all* -- or whatever.   It's a feeling much like missing the million dollar jackpot by one pull of the slot handle.   SO close....and yet so far...   And you have to sit there and be big about it, and tell them everything'll work out for them, and even go so far as to HELP them on their way whenever possible – knowing that it's absolutely *killing* you inside.   But it's worth it – because nothing would make you happier than seeing them be happy – even at your own expense.

You'd do anything for them – you would literally die for them because your life has little meaning without them. That person has become your holy grail – now an object, so desired it couldn't *possibly* live up to your expectations!

I suppose everyone has one of those – a person who's totally in love with you, but never tells you.   As far as I know, I've never had one, but I guess *knowing* would invalidate the statement, so...

We all want what we can not have, and tend to *not* want that which we do have.   But then, you don't know what you've got until it's gone!

It's a dirty little mess, isn't it? And there's no solution. Everybody hurts. The only way to win the game is not to play, and what fun is that? The only people who are truly happy in relationships are those too shallow to care about the fact that they may be lacking something. Seriously. Sucks, doesn't it? Maybe that's just me being jaded. Maybe that's the result of being with the same person – the only person – for so many years. But then, I was *never* really happy in this relationship – and *neither was she*. We were both just too afraid to be alone anymore, and I guess that's worth something. Panic reaction - but it's better than nothing at all. Except when it's not. It's a delicate line to walk.

The truth may simply be that human beings aren't meant to bond with one another permanently. If you grow apart, you should be free to drift apart without artificial constructs and man-made laws getting in the way.

I know, I signed up for this deal, and I'm not complaining. I'm warning others – think ahead, and not just about how you feel *right now*. No matter how bad you may feel over the loss of this one, or the next one, or 15 people down the line.

Eventually, someone will come along who feels that way about *you* – as much as you feel that way about *them,* and *then* you'll know you're in the right place. At least, I hope so. I'm still waiting. So are you. Is everyone? No wonder the world is such a fucked up, filthy place to live...

Just tonight, my wife and I had another long discussion. So long, it caused her to call in sick for work, in fact. Among other things, I had to ask;

"Do you know that tingly feeling you get when you hug that special person?"

"Yes?"

"Do you feel that way when we're together?"

"….not really…."

…and neither do I. So what the hell are we doing here? Seriously. We both agreed that we've *had* that electric, awesome, body tingling on fire feeling when hugging another person – just that it wasn't with each other! There's something incredibly wrong with that, but it has convinced me that things can't be as black and white as they've seemed. Once again, she told me she wouldn't be *too* upset if I was with another woman. ONE other woman. Not jumping from bed to bed. Just doing what I need to do with someone who makes me feel special.

It's a goddamned shame that I don't feel that way with my wife. Tonight she confirmed my suspicion that she doesn't feel that way with me. I think the only reason she sticks around is because of what I do for her in bed. THAT she *likes* – the rest of the day, not so much.

So I'm going to do it. I'm going to do what I want, if I get an opportunity. And I'm *not* going to feel guilty. Because there's really nothing wrong with it. There's really nothing wrong with *me*. I'm not an old man. I'm not ready to die. I have a LONG time left on this planet.

There's no reason to spend it all unhappy. Or less happy. Or whatever. I have to find out. She understands this. She *needs* me to find out. She might not like it, but I guarantee she doesn't want to keep dealing with this for the next 50 years.

Would I leave my wife for someone else? Yes. I'm sorry. I would. Positively. But only for the absolute right person. I even know who it *might* be. If I ever find out I'm right, we'll deal with it. Until then, business as usual – with a little extra time spent thinking of being happy – and smiling. No time is being spent planning or plotting though. No practicing potential conversations. No going over things in my head a thousand times. No plans whatsoever. I'm going to take things as they come, and see what happens, and live life for the first time ever. If I get what I want, fucking amazing! My entire world will change forever – inside and out.

If I don't – or I never say anything else about it – my brain will change forever. No matter what I decide, or what the universe wants – there's *going* to be a change in my future. Soon. A change that might affect the futures of a lot of people I love – but perhaps for the better.

What if doing the one thing I truly want could change the course of events in such a way as to make all our dreams come true? Possible? In the words of the immortal Cliff Burton,

"Abso-mother-fucking-lutely!"

Don't argue with Cliff, people! Not a wise choice. In fact, beware of *all* zombified musicians. Seriously, though. I wonder – if we're both on the same wavelength (there's a 50/50 chance, I suppose) -- what WOULD happen?

What would happen......

So many possibilities. Are any of them positive? Heck yeah! I can think of a hundred amazing futures that involve the two of us – and Tommy, of course. I can also think of another, more likely future – and that *doesn't* bother me. I'm not holding onto any delusions. I'm not convincing myself of anything. I'm believing only what I hear directly from the source.

Numbers, words, suppositions – none of these mean anything. Only the words I hear directly from her mouth – and the words I speak with mine. Nothing else matters. *No more* hiding behind the written word. It's time for face to face speaking. It's time to talk it out, and get to know one another, if that's our destiny.

If not, we'll figure that out too.   No more details for you! I'm not ready to tip my hat...   If you're *really* smart, you're already on to me, you bastard!   I know at least two people who are laughing out loud at me *right this very instant*.   Aren't you? Yes.... YOU!   I love both of you as well....   You're among my closest confidants!   You know, there are less than 10 people in the entire world that know much of *anything* about me.   *That's all...*

"Some of you might not agree

cause you probably likes a lot of misery

But think a while and you will see...

Broken hearts are for assholes"

Life truly *is* the giant rollercoaster I was once told it was –
a series of peaks and valleys. When you're on top of the
world and feeling great, you're *about* to be heading
downhill fast, but when you get there, you *immediately*
start climbing back up. And so on. Forever. -- but
that's how it is, so you do what you have to.

You feel like you're not trying hard enough? For who?
For you, yes? If so, why not? What do YOU think you
should be doing? What do YOU WANT to be doing?
Where do you want to be? It IS all about you, because
you're the *only* one who can behave that way! *You* have
to take care of *you* first, or no one else can be much help.

You want to get out of here - *and go where*? And do
what? It's no better anywhere else. Running won't
help.

Bad things happen to good people all the fucking time. I
hate to have to be the one to lift that particular veil,
because it's there for comfort. It doesn't work that
way…. Take a look at all the people that really good
things happen to. Common thread - they're usually
pieces of shit. Now look at the people who've sacrificed
themselves in many ways and tried to do good for the
world. Broke, starving, imprisoned, killed, etc etc.
"Gee, thanks! That cheered me right up!" If I was
always positive, you'd know I was full of shit, right? I'm
not. I have no reason to fill your head with any
additional bullshit.

In brief, the best people I've ever known have been the first ones to die - all the way down the line.

There was a Denis Leary joke (which he *probably* borrowed from Bill Hicks...) "Stevie Ray Vaughan died in a plane crash – but we can't *get* Bon Jovi to a fucking airport!" As in, the good die young, while the mediocre flourish. Happy thought, eh? So fuck it. Nothing you can do about it anyway.

Live for today. Live for yourself. Just make sure and LIVE. Don't lock yourself away inside yourself like I had to. You should hear the noise that guy makes trying to get out of there. It's not pretty. I keep hoping for the kiss that never comes -- like that frog that turned into Prince!

No wait, he turned into - A - prince. He'd be cooler with the little mustache and purple guitar. Whatever. One of these days, I'm just going to steal it. Wouldn't kill me...

Shitty is a frame of mind. It's all in what you make of what you've got. I have my moments when I'd like to just...do....something! To escape - to get away - to not be in my head - in this house - repeating the same drill again and again. It would be all too easy to just give up. Then I see Tommy and I remember he's still got a chance - and he needs my help. So I'm good... All the other stuff will come in time. You just have to hold on and keep believing - and don't lose track of the goal along the way!

I had a childhood, I never made it out. I'm *still* stuck deep within my childhood. Anytime you need to, well, feel childish, I'm your guy! You know what I mean. I'm good at connecting with inner children. It's adults that fuck me over!

There's still plenty of time for everything. That's one of the things that writing all my crap down has done for me.

It made me realize that while time is limited, and you shouldn't dwell on things forever, time is also *flexible*, and you may wake up years down the road to realize that everything you've ever wanted is right there with you.

I woke up to realize that everything I want is nearby – is within reach, so I decided it was about fucking time to start reaching. And I do. The brain issues are nothing new, I don't have to think about or deal with that. It just happens. Other than big problem #1, the rest of the stuff I deal with isn't too bad. I would have myself completely under control if I could just answer my few remaining questions. Grrr, Argh... Oh well. You know how it goes.

I'll keep reaching, though.

If you're keeping things inside, only YOU can deal with them. Remember that, and you should be ok. I could say things that would make you feel better in one direction and worse in another. That's pointless as can be.

You wouldn't listen anyway. Or you wouldn't believe me. And there's no point in it anyway, because at the end of the day, you're going to have to struggle through those rough years like everyone else does, and it's going to suck. It'll all work out... You're just going to have to be strong – *and you are.* You're one of the strongest people I know. Believe.

As for me, whatever happens, I'm not going to kid myself with any of my old nonsense. There are no signs, hints, omens, or signals. Nothing. There is only that which you *do* – and that which happens in response. I'm done thinking about it – and I'm done worrying. It's time to make things happen for myself – or shut the fuck up.

I must admit, I *have* made something of a deal though. See, there is something I want *so* badly right now, that is *so* unlikely to ever happen, yet strangely possible, if that makes sense. Anyway, I looked up the other day and thought, "There's never been anything to demonstrate to me, or make me think that there's anything out there that's in control of anything, or looking out for me, or whatever." I don't know exactly what I believe. Essentially, I think the universe knows what it needs to do to survive, and does it's best to set the environment up to ensure it. Much like an ant farm, or a bee hive – only made up of galaxies, and planets, etc. The biggest eco-sphere you could possibly imagine.

So while I feel that there may be an order to things, I don't picture an old bearded man in a robe pointing his finger at things and making it happen. Without getting uber-geek, it seems more like the Force – the good spirits pouring forth from good people help other people do good things and so on and so on. Much like I described the concept of being a musician earlier.

Where was I? Yes, regardless of what I believe, if that which I seek comes to pass – I *SWEAR* to you all, right here and now, I *WILL* believe there is something out there, because I used to ask for something – night after night after night - for 10 years or more - with no result – and I've just recently asked again (thus making the deal we're discussing.) I haven't had a *reason* to ask in a decade. I haven't had a reason to do anything, really.

If it happens, there's no other explanation my rational mind would accept *other* than there being something out there that is able to assist, shape, guide, or even determine the results and events that take place in the universe. You read it right here, folks. And I'm being totally serious.

If it happens, there *is* a God. Absolutely. OK?

"When it feels like these walls are crashing down

I'll fall to pieces – but I'll put myself together again."

Right this very minute, I'm having two separate conversations with two members of my band – my two best friends in the world, my two kindred souls – and we're all totally excited about the future! How strange is that? For a person who tries never to think about the future to be *excited* about the future? Wow! It's amazing from the inside out!

We're *going* to make it this time, you see. I've been through all this before. I've seen the mistakes. I've seen the problems. I've seen people screw up and lose everything. Throw away all their friends – their values – their souls for money, or fame, or acceptance, or whatever the fuck it was they were after in the moment. I've lived this life already, though with a different mind. This time, the person in control has already seen the game – knows all the plays – can anticipate the opposition and easily step around it. There is simply no conflict this time. We have it all. We have what is going to be needed desperately in two years. We will be *incredibly* good at what we do in two years. The right place at the right fucking time. Finally... You have no idea how long it's taken. Then again, how old am I? Not very. Maybe I'm right on schedule. It's just that my brain is moving at hyperspeed! I have no idea how much longer I have. I want to get there while I still have time to enjoy it. Even if I don't, I can take some comfort in knowing that my band will get there.

Can you imagine how it will feel the moment I can look up and see all four of them living their lives happy and relatively carefree? "Finally Happy" indeed… Goddamn it, that's what keeps me breathing. That, and everything that Thomas does.

I talked to my stepmother Donna the other day. She'd heard about my visit to my dad when she got home from vacation, and had a lot of stuff on her mind. She reminded me about the first time we met – on the day my grandfather died back in 1981.

"Actually, if I am not mistaken, the first time I met you was to babysit, because your grandfather had died. I had all of these grand plans of taking you to Assumption-Grotto. They were having a carnival. You just kind of cowered in your bedroom. I felt just awful."

Wow. I DO remember that moment. I *hadn't*, until she mentioned it. She's had the thought that it had something to do with *her*, for all these years? I'll bet I can help. First of all, no one ever knew about the voices, or apparently wondered why I used to sit in the closet in the dark and talk to myself, so that was certainly a big factor in that behavior. What she's never heard *anything* about are the events that preceded that moment in time.

I'm seven years old. Two hours ago, I just learned about death for the first time. One of my favorite people in the entire world was gone forever, and I was in the process of trying to understand what that meant. Especially with my reality issues – and the fact that I could still hear his voice in my head, talking to me. I still can. The following sequence is as close as I can come to correct, having to estimate the parts I wasn't directly involved in.

My mom had to go up north with my grandma, and they didn't want to put a little kid through that. She called my dad, who was still at work. He'd be home later though, so I could certainly sleep over there. What to do with me in the meantime? Options being extremely limited, I had to go to Nana and Grandpa's. These were my great-grandparents – my *grandmother's* mother and stepfather. Why was this a "last resort"? This guy was no prize... He'd had a long history of doing *wildly* inappropriate things (and then some) with kids. Neighbor kids, family kids, *any kids* close by. They'd all been through this in some way or another. Not a good place to leave your seven year old son. That must've been an impossible moment. Whatever. I'd be OK!

Sure enough, within a half hour, he asked me into the back room to get some toys. What followed is probably the coolest thing my smart assed mouth ever did for me.

He pulls it out and says "Do you know what *this* is?"

I said "Sure! It's just like my dad's! Only small and wrinkly!"

He put it away and gave me some crayons and sent me out to watch television with Nana.

Take that, motherfucker. Shot down and depowered by a *seven year old* who just didn't give a fuck – even then. *Especially then.* I'd just learned that nothing fucking mattered on earth.

I was never traumatized by the experience. Nothing happened! I've always found that moment funny, more than anything. Lots of other people were hurt in more extreme ways, so I've never fully shared that story. It didn't hurt me. It was entertaining. *I fucked his mind like no one ever had.* And he *hated* me the rest of his useless, miserable life for it. Anyone who ever wondered just *why* he hated me *so* much knows as of now...

Less than ten minutes later, while I was drawing on the living room floor, my cousin Sandy shows up at the door to pick me up. They were all quite eager to get me out of there. Mom must've gotten a hold of Sandy (who likely went through her own abuse, I'd imagine) and sent her over to save her kid before it was too late. Too late. Missed it by ten minutes. Amazing, isn't it? I'd *love* to see what I was drawing!

Regardless, Sandy got me (and herself) the hell out of there immediately. It was raining SO hard at that moment, I remember she had to pull over because she couldn't see to drive. We weren't going home. She was taking me to Dad's house! That would work. Dad was living in our old house at that point. My old bedroom was there! A safe place! *Somewhere I can go and sit and hide out* – away from the world – away from these people who are freaking me out – away from everything – and just hide!

Dad wasn't there yet! I'd imagine the conversation went something like;

"Go pick him up at Nana's as soon as you can."

"Nana's! You left him over there with THEM?"

"I had no other option!"

"Jesus Christ! My girlfriend should be home from work by now. He's going to have to meet her sooner or later. Might as well be now. It's better than leaving him over *there*!"

Then she frantically searched for someone to get me out of there – and succeeded!   So, I get taken to my old house, and my cousin takes me in, and introduces me to my "babysitter", Donna.

I have *no* idea what's going on in my world right now. Every adult I've seen since dinner time has been either crying hysterically, trying to molest me, or BOTH. Fun. I'm being escorted around by someone I don't know well enough to blindly trust, and being left in a safe place – but with a total stranger! Hmm.

I did the *only* thing I could do – I went in my room, and hid away from the world, and attempted to *save myself* from going entirely insane from all the questions that were flying around inside my head.

See, Donna... It had nothing to do with you. You were just there at the wrong moment. Or maybe the right moment, because if you *weren't* there, who knows? Crazy old fucker might've taken me downstairs and *killed* me. I never did trust that tool area in the back of their basement. Neither did any of the other kids – ask them. I've never disliked you, or resented you or anything of the sort. You've always been cool to me! C'mon... you were the first one to bring video games into the house! How could you be anything less than awesome to a seven year old? Plus, you listened to cool music that Dad usually hated! For the record, while I'm getting all this out there – I did NOT – *DID NOT* – spit on you on purpose after we saw Return of the Jedi. Friday, May 27, 1983, and I've been pissed about it ever since. I get really serious dry mouth when I'm pissed or scared. We were arguing, I WAS mad, *and freaking out*, and I spit to clear the cotton ball out of my mouth so I could talk. I swear today – *as I did then* – the glob hit the breeze and diverted in your direction. Total accident. No one *EVER* believed me. Disappointed the shit out of me, and taught me that the truth wasn't always the answer. Oops. Backfired, eh?

Whatever happened to the old people responsible for all the misery? They got older, made a lot of people more miserable, ruined my grandmother's final years, destroyed each other, and died unhappy, alone, miserable, lost, scared, and confused.

My grandmother is gone, so I can tell you this.   When Nana died, that man *dragged her around town* for several days.   He took her out to dinner.   He took her to Sears.   The police called, someone had reported a man dragging a body around at the mall.   She had difficulty walking, he frequently did things like that.   My grandmother had talked to "them" the night before.   He told her that her mother was angry with him over something.   He didn't know why – she wouldn't talk to him.   She wouldn't come to the phone either.   She simply wasn't going to say anything, she was so angry. *I know why...*

Next day, we get another call.   The old man had backed the car through the garage door.   The cops had arrived, and found old dead Nana in the passenger seat.   Decaying.   In the heat of the garage.

One of two things happened that day.   Either he had gotten so fed up, he decided to end it all, and hauled her dead bones out to the car to monoxide away in a closed garage.   If that happened, he panicked, and crashed through the door to live.

What I think happened was more like, he loaded her into the car to go to Kmart, bitching about it the entire time.

"Goddamnit, Ann, I don't know *why* you won't talk to me! This is getting ridiculous!"

Then, when he got himself into the car, the dumb fuck forgot to push the 'door open' button – he'd always had a world of trouble with any sort of button, or switch, or electronic device.   He'd forgotten to open the door and driven through it and gotten trapped until the cops showed to pull him out *and found him in the car with a very dead corpse*.

We got to the hospital about 20 minutes later.   Nana was *decayed and stiff* - as if she'd been dead for three or four *days*.   I wonder why *that* was?   Nice, eh?   They thought about charging him with a crime, but what? Senility?   It didn't matter.   The opportunity passed, he went on to a rest home somewhere in the middle of nowhere (after fucking up one last time for good measure and signing the hundreds of thousands they'd greeded away over the years off to his shady health care person, who came in one day and saw opportunity knocking.   He got married again at 89 years old, weeks after his wife died and he had played "Weekend at Bernie's - the Home Game", signed off everything he had for the promise of a blowjob and had it all taken away from him.

Any family he *had* wanted nothing else to do with him. He was a miserable prick his entire life.   His money was gone. Hello, shitty state provided care until the day you rot completely away!   Worse than prison -- he wouldn't get to *enjoy* it.   He *must* be dead by now.   I think.   Took him long enough... Only the good die young, right?

One thing I seem to have a hard time remembering – my brain ALWAYS finds a way for me to win before the game is completely over. It's *never* failed me. It just responds differently than it used to… I can still do any damned thing I set my mind to.

Watch me.

"Ooh ooh woo hoo, Jackie Blue - has a dream that can never come true…"

It would appear to anyone watching that every day in every way I am getting better and better. A *million* bonus points to anyone who gets that reference (even Google can't help, I promise! The *obvious* answer is the *incorrect* answer.) - but it's true!   The more I try to convince myself I can't do something, the more something convinces me that I *can*.   I had a fucking moment of joy, the kind I haven't felt in a long time. And it came from doing something totally silly, and actually had a silly consequence that made me feel terrible for a second, then I was like "fuck it!" and it became funny for no reason.   What was this odd sensation? Fun? Happy? Comfort in the presence of others? Wait…what? *Comfort in the presence of others?* Surely not!   But yeah – and at some point, I even violated my personal space rules.   Oddly enough, everyone in that room has personal space rules, but we all seemed comfy enough together. I wonder why?

Also, as a total non-sequitur to get me out of this line of conversation, I noticed yet again that Adam acts really nervous at the mention of divorce. This isn't the first time.   I don't know if he thinks he's keeping me from making a mistake (without knowing he's years too late) or *what* the deal is.

It's not THAT big a deal, but come to think of it, one of my major, *major* issues would've already come to an end (or changed into a *new* issue, at least) one night months ago, but he put himself in the way to keep me from "doing something stupid." Hmm... I wasn't going to do what he *thought* I was trying to do – not at all!

But I was about ¼" away from *finally finding out* what another girl's lips tasted like when he jumped up and got in the way. *Like he was trying to take a bullet for me.* Bastard! I wished I *had* one for him at that moment! I'm not bitching though, I have a feeling he's doing it out of love – he doesn't want to see me throw it all away - or something. But he doesn't know the whole story – or the truth. Yet.

Besides, for all this typing and revising, it's the words left unwritten between the lines that I'm burning to say the most. If I'm not careful, someone's going to read them anyway, and then what? Hey, if you can read between *these* lines, then the message is meant for you anyway, so you win! The rest of you can continue to babble contentedly while we who are in on the joke giggle uncontrollably - at your expense. In the immortal words of Nelson, "Ha, Ha!"

Of course, the easiest solution to the whole mess is to go all Obi-Wan Kenobi, raise my arms, and let it strike me down. Somehow, I don't think I would become more powerful than Vader could possibly imagine, though. I'd probably be a babbling, drooling idiot in this reality.

My brain would be in a happier place though.   I can picture it now, as clear as necessary.   Then I think, and it fades...   I can't describe it to you, as it would reveal a bit too much.   I *can* describe my former dreamspace for you instead if that makes you feel any better.

Before my dreams were stolen and locked away, I used to be a seriously lucid dreamer.   For those who are unfamiliar, it's basically the ability to control your dreams from within.

The knowledge that you are dreaming *while* you are dreaming allows your mind to reshape your dreams to your liking – and allows your brain to feel like it's had those experiences and be a bit more content.   Don't like the dream?   Change it.   Having a nightmare?   Wake yourself up.   Or better yet, TAKE CONTROL AND FIX EVERYTHING.

Oh shit.   Is THAT what's going on here?   Is that why it's been so much worse lately?   All the freedom I used to get from dreams – mentally and spiritually – was GONE. Nowhere to be found.   Am I seeking out things in the real world I used to be content to merely dream about?

Goddamned right!   And I'm going to continue, too.   It's that whole quest for knowledge thing.   I NEED to know – if only to confirm there's nothing to my theory.   Blame the scientist in me.

I've only ever described my dreamspace to one person. The place where I would go, in my mind, while falling asleep. From there I could manifest any dream I desired, and wander around freely within. I frequently miss specific years from the past. I could go back there any time I was asleep – seeing, hearing, smelling all the same stuff I had in the first place. It was as close to being there as one could ever hope for. Though I could never fucking *touch* anything.

That was the limitation. If I even *tried* to touch, I would be thrown from the dream. Ever have that feeling that you're falling fast, and you wake up and you've just "landed" in bed? And the bed is still shaking like you jerked the hell out of it?

That's you, being forcibly ejected from whatever you were dreaming up, only you don't remember the fun (or frightening) part that caused the disconnect.

I'm not kidding – it's your brain acting as an alarm clock to prevent your psyche from getting fucked by dream events -- the real world analogy to the "die in your dream and you'll die in real life from the shock" myth. It's a myth, guaranteed, because I can't count the number of times I've been murdered in cold blood in a dream, felt the pain, seen the world fade to white – and immediately jerked awake. If my brain is *supposed* to be waking me earlier, *it's not* – it's having a little fun with me first.

Dreaming of being shot in the face – and feeling it as if it were "real" – is simply not fun.   And it would only happen as a pop-up moment – a sudden event. No time to shift lanes or rearrange events. No time to make any decision at all. Usually, just…BANG! Sometimes I'd stay asleep, and lay there slowly dying before deciding it was ok to wake myself up.   If you're into symbolism, you've found your paragraph!

While dreaming, I could be anywhere I'd ever been – or seen – or imagined!   I was never someone else in my dreams – never looked better than I really did, or any of the self-delusional stuff.   No, I was simply free.   To do what I want.   Any old time.   I could try out entire conversations while I slept!   Had to talk to someone difficult tomorrow?   Dream it up tonight, see what works, what doesn't work, wake up and take notes, repeat.   In the morning, you'll have your answer. No wonder I feel so lost lately. *I'm shut out of myself.*

The doors have been locked since a few months before Thomas was born.   First, the sleeping got disturbed – initially by having to lay next to a seriously pregnant woman in a seriously broken bed. I highly recommend not trying this, if at all possible.   Then he was born, and there was no sleep for anyone.   15 minute naps were considered a treat.   No way in hell was I going to get 4 hours deep enough to go into REM sleep.

I don't know who I may have left in there, but they're probably starving for something by now. Maybe some of this extra need for experience is them trying to get through to me. Whispering – begging - SCREAMING for me to get them the hell out of there – to set them free.

I had to put the place in the back of my head for the time being, until I could sort it all out. I was stunned when I saw Pan's Labyrinth for the first time, and *there was my dream room*! When the little girl walks down the stone spiral staircase into the damp dark stone room, she's walking into my dreamspace – EXACTLY as it's always appeared in my head. Though that cool Faun doesn't live in MY room...

The one person I've ever fully described it to is likely reading this - I say to her, if you haven't seen that movie, go do so. Is that exactly what I described way back when, or what?

That was one of the weirdest feelings in the world. To someone who has frequent questions about what exactly is real and what is not, seeing something that came from deep within my imagination and my self on a 40 ft screen was really hard to wrap my mind around, and yet somehow, they had *nailed* it!

Nice job! Now get the fuck out of my head before you get trapped in here forever with the rest of us.

Each day that I wake up, I face the same struggle. Some days, it's not too bad. Some days, it's all I can do to lift my head and keep my eyes open. I never know which way it's going to go, until it's going.

One of our recent gigs made me realize that I'm certainly not getting any *better*. I was in a supremely good mood. Things were going great. Within 30 seconds, something caused a mood swing. 10 minutes later, something made it worse. 15 minutes after that, I was devastated, 5 seconds later, I was ok. 30 seconds after that, I was trying to get away from people in case I broke down. I didn't. I very rarely do. I made it through the entire show - wanting to get the hell out of there the entire time. It might've been the freaky light show they had going in there, but I noticed I didn't even want to look up to see what the band was doing. Not because I was mad at *them* or anything – just because it was SO hard to lift my head up and keep my eyes open. I leaned on a wall, head down, eyes closed, fidgeting with my hair for 90 minutes. I haven't had a shoegazing moment like that in YEARS. Why now?

After the show comes the parking lot chaos. I never know what to do with myself. I want to help them load up and pack stuff – or sell merch – or *whatever*. Instead, I try to find a place to hide – to be out of the way – *to lurk*. As things are getting worse, several people do several things to toss me over the edge.

Not on purpose! Not by trying to be evil. No, these people are doing nothing but being nice and friendly, and I'm going insane. Why now?

Then Adam starts in. A) because he's drunk at this point, and B) because I haven't been to his house yet. I guess he thinks I'm avoiding him or something. Not true. *You* know that, from reading to this point. He doesn't. He will...and he's going to feel like *such* a dick! Didn't matter. We worked it out. Still made me feel like shit though. I was right on the brink of full-on panic when Crystal caught what was going on and stepped in and pulled me back down. She knows how to do so. She's good like that. It's nice having backup. That's one of the main reasons I'm letting people in. Keeping it secret isn't helping me deal with anything. In fact, it makes it worse because I have to keep coming up with new and greater excuses. I love it when someone asks if I'm "in trouble" at home – like I'm *really* leaving because my wife said so. If you ever believed that, my acting chops are *still* there. Nope. *100% of the time*, when I say I have a phone call, or I have to be somewhere at a certain time, or that I've got "stuff to do" – I'm LYING. L Y I N G -- Telling non-truths.

Come on! I *don't* answer the phone – I *don't* deal with ultimatums, I *don't* do what people tell me, and you think I'm running out on you because someone calls? *That'll make me drop everything and run?* If something was wrong with Thomas, absolutely!

Otherwise? *Once or twice a day for years?* Think about it. Wookies don't live on Endor, my friend.

The other big reason I pull out of parties at the last minute is that *I don't fully trust myself anymore.* Not when our old friend, Cap'n Morgan is around. A little goes a long way towards making me able to look at and talk to people. Doesn't take much. Problem is, once those inhibitions are shut down, watch out!

I'm telling you, there *will* come a day when I'm drinking, and lots of these hot, sweaty, pheromone radiating, possibly available, possibly willing, certainly beautiful girls will be there too, and we'll be having fun, and I'll just say "what the fuck" and... and...? Move! Try! Do something! REACH!

Hell, I already did that once! Felt terrible about it too. We were all pretty 'out of control wasted' at that point. It was a special occasion, there were lots of people around. It was a 2 second thing. I walked through a room, and squeezed someone as a joke – not in a touchy feely prolonged manner, just a quick whoops, right? Here's where I sober up enough to go "Whoa! That wasn't my wife! I'm not supposed to do *that*!" I picked the *wrong* girl, too.

Before I could finish the thought, I have Adam in my face telling me that I'm behaving improperly and can't do stuff like that. I *just* figured that out on my own, bud, but thanks!

It wasn't what he said, as much as the fact that he felt it *needed* to be said. Maybe it did. I'm *sure* it did from his point of view. Remember, we'd only known each other a few months at that point. It was natural for him to be protective. I *could've* been that music industry predator guy who runs around with dozens of young chicks and throws them aside. He didn't know. *They* didn't know. I'm sure the girl was freaked out at the moment and went to him and - I don't know what.

Doesn't matter. I've apologized for it since. It really wasn't meant to be a big deal, but things have a way of blowing out of proportion real quick. He kept being in my way the rest of that night. I don't know what had gotten into me that day...

I was on a mission, apparently -- or maybe just past my frustration saturation point. Meanwhile, he's banging his girlfriend on the couch – and behind the couch – and wherever else they might've been at the moment the mood struck them. I don't know where he found time to babysit me.

Are we going to go through this *every time*? Are we going to be out on the road in the middle of nowhere, and I'm going to have this guy running around blocking every opportunity I put the extreme effort into setting up? I won't be touring long, if that's the case.

I told him - the week we decided to make an album –

"Of course, when it's all over, in addition to owing me your immortal souls (or what's left of 'em) and billions upon billions of dollars, I expect several rounds of intoxication and debauchery (which I'm told is a band specialty....hehe)"

Don't believe me? Check your mail, bro - 7/26/06!

And - his response –

"Believe me dude, when this is all said and done... well, you know what they say, sex, drugs, and rock n' roll.... we owe you our souls and more than one rowdy night."

He already *knew* I was married. He'd met my wife years before. He knew about Thomas, because he'd spent all that time in the Library with Tom Starks, who not only got us all together in the first place, but helped provide the name for my child. Adam *knows* my situation – knows what my *true* motivations are – knows *why* I'm in it -- why does he act so surprised?

Lucky for all of us, we still have plenty of time. It's nowhere near over. *We're only getting warmed up.* Oh, and the thing with their souls? I don't want to own them -- I want to *free* them.

Hey, thanks for making it all the way to the end! Hope you're not expecting any closure! I can't provide what I don't have. Prepare yourself for the Sopranos ending, reader-person, because I'm not finishing the final sentence of this book. You're going to have to *choose your own* word to fill in the blank. Person, place, or thing? One noun can make all the difference in the world. Use your imaginations, there are *millions* of possible answers, but only one of them is correct. You can think about it forever, but you'll never *really* know the *true* answer. It makes little difference whether I confirm or deny your suspicions. You'll never know if I'm being honest or not! The answer isn't written down anywhere, so there's nothing preventing me from *changing* it on the fly. There are so many possible choices, that there can never be a solution. Which gives you all a little more insight into what it's like to be me. At this point, I truly *don't* know what tomorrow brings, and I *really* don't care. So here's a sudden lack of wrapping up (because there's *always* more to come) and a last second *tease* at my big Unanswered Question before the credits roll. Picture it as the end scene in a movie that presumes you'll want to see the eventual sequel. Scene fades out on a close up of a face in a dark, smoky room -- voiceover reads:

*Anyone who knows me – the **real** me – only need close their eyes and imagine - it only takes 5 seconds to visualize an image – to realize her name is*

I would die for you
I've been dying just to feel you by my side
To know that you're mine

I will cry for you
I will wash away your pain with all my tears
And drown your fear

I will pray for you
I will sell my soul for something pure and true
Someone like you

See your face every place that I walk in
Hear your voice every time that I'm talking
You will believe in me
And I will never be ignored

I will burn for you, Feel pain for you
I will twist the knife and bleed my aching heart
And tear it apart

I will lie for you, Beg and steal for you
I will crawl on hands and knees until you see
You're just like me

Violate all the love that I'm missing
Throw away all the pain that I'm living
You will believe in me
And I can never be ignored

I would die for you

I would kill for you

I will steal for you

I'd do time for you

I will wait for you

I'd make room for you

I'd sink ships for you

To be close to you

To be part of you

I believe in you

I would die for you

Who can it be knocking at my door
Go away, don't come 'round here no more
Can't you see that it's late at night
I'm very tired, and I'm not feeling right

All I wish is to be alone
Stay away, don't you invade my home
Best off if you hang outside
Don't come in - I'll only run and hide

Who can it be, knocking at my door
Make no sound, tip-toe across the floor
If he hears, he'll knock all day
I'll be trapped, and here I'll have to stay

I've done no harm, I keep to myself
There's nothing wrong with my state of mental health
I like it here with my childhood friend
Here they come - those feelings again!

Is it the man? Come to take me away?
Why do they follow me?
It's not the future that I can see
It's just my fantasy...

Avalanche is sullen and too thin
She starves herself to rid herself of sin
And the kick is so divine when she sees bones beneath
her skin
And she says:
Hey baby can you bleed like me?
C'mon baby can you bleed like me

Chris is all dressed up and acting coy
Painted like a brand new Christmas toy
He's trying to figure out if he's a girl or he's a boy
He says:
Hey baby can you bleed like me?
C'mon baby can you bleed like me

Doodle takes Dad's scissors to her skin
And when she does relief comes setting in
While she hides the scars she's making underneath her
pretty clothes
She sings:
Hey baby can you bleed like me?
C'mon baby can you bleed like me

Therapy is Speedie's brand new drug
Dancing with the devil's past has never been too fun
It's better off than trying to take a bullet from a gun
And she cries:
Hey baby can you bleed like me?
C'mon baby can you bleed like me

JT gets all fucked up in some karaoke bar
After two drinks he's a loser, after three drinks

he's a star

Getting all nostalgic as he sings "I Will Survive"
Hey baby can you bleed like me?
C'mon baby can you bleed like me
Hey baby can you bleed like me?
Oh, c'mon baby can you bleed like me

You should see my scars
You should see my scars
You should see my scars
You should see my scars

And try to comprehend that which you'll never
comprehend
Try to comprehend that which you'll never comprehend
Just try to comprehend that which you'll never
comprehend
Try to comprehend that which you'll never comprehend

You should see my scars
You should see my scars

This world rejects me
This world threw me away
This world never gave me a chance
This world gonna have to pay

Well I don't believe in your institutions
I did what you wanted me to
I'm like the cancer in your system
I've got a little surprise for you

Something inside of me
Has opened up its eyes
Why did you put it there?
Did you not realize
This thing inside of me
It screams the loudest sound
Sometimes I think I could

Burn...

I look down at where you're standing
Flock of sheep out on display
With all your lies bumped up around you
I can take it all away

Something inside of me
Has opened up its eyes
Why did you put it there?
Did you not realize
Something inside of me

It screams the loudest sound
Sometimes I think I could

I'm gonna burn this whole world down...

I never was a part of you...

Burn...

I was a soldier

I am corruption

I am the agent

Of your destruction

I am perversion

Sick with desire

I am your future

Swallowed up in fire

You love her but she loves him

And he loves somebody else, you just can't win
And so it goes, til the day you die...

I beat my machine it's a part of me it's inside of me
I'm stuck in this dream it's changing me I am becoming
the me that you know, he had some second thoughts
he's covered with scabs and he is broken and sore
the me that you know, he doesn't come around much
that   part   of   me   *isn't   here   anymore*
all pain disappears it's the nature of my circuitry
drowns out all I hear there's no escape from this

my   new   consciousness
the   me   that   you   know   used   to   have   feelings
but the blood has stopped pumping and he's left to
decay
the me that you know is now made up of wires
and even when I'm right with you I'm so far away
I can try to get away but I've strapped myself in
I can try to scratch away the sound in my ears
I can see it killing away all of my bad parts
I don't want to listen but it's all too clear

hiding backwards inside of me I feel so unafraid
Annie, hold a little tighter I might just slip away

Itwontgiveupitwantsmedeadandgoddamnthisnoiseinsidemyhead

Itwontgiveupitwantsmedeadandgoddamnthisnoiseinsidemyhead

Itwontgiveupitwantsmedeadandgoddamnthisnoiseinsidemyhead

Itwontgiveupitwantsmedeadandgoddamnthisnoiseinsidemyhead

Itwontgiveupitwantsmedeadandgoddamnthisnoiseinsidemyhead